SPOTLIGHT ON LITERACY

SPELLING
ACTIVITY BOOK

Grade 2

Macmillan
McGraw-Hill

New York • Farmington

CONTENTS

LEVEL 6, UNIT 1

LEVEL 6, UNIT 2

/ī/ -ight, -y

Pretest Directions

Fold back your paper along the dotted line. Use the blanks to write each word as it is said to you. When you finish the test, unfold the paper and correct any spelling mistakes. Practice those words for the Final Test.

To Parents,

Here are the results of your child's weekly spelling Pretest. You can help your child study for the Final Test by following these simple steps for each word on the word list:

1. Read the word to your child.
2. Have your child write the word, saying each letter as it is written.
3. Say each letter of the word as your child checks the spelling.
4. If a mistake has been made, have your child read each letter of the correctly spelled word aloud and then repeat steps 1–3.

Parent/Child Activity: As you study the list of words, have your child find and spell the letter patterns used to spell the long **i** sound in the lesson. Reread a familiar book together to discover and spell words with the long *i* sound you hear in the *ight* of *right* or the *y* in *try*.

1. _____	1. night
2. _____	2. right
3. _____	3. why
4. _____	4. flight
5. _____	5. might
6. _____	6. tight
7. _____	7. slight
8. _____	8. fright
9. _____	9. try
10. _____	10. sky
Challenge Words	Challenge Words
_____	who
_____	whose

Macmillan/McGraw-Hill

/ī/-ight, -y

Sound Off

Your spelling words show two ways to spell the long **i** sound.

Write the letters that have the long **i** sound in the shapes below.

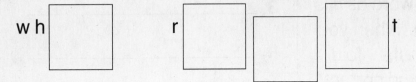

w h ⬜   r ⬜ ⬜ t

A Path Home

Help Hattie the Cat find her way home.

Trace the path made by words with the long **i** sound spelled **-y**.

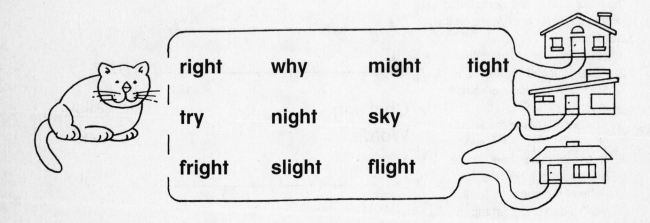

right	why	might	tight
try	night	sky	
fright	slight	flight	

Macmillan/McGraw-Hill

/ī/ -ight, -y

So You Say

Write the spelling words that complete each thought.

1. The _____ is blue.

2. There is a _____ chance of rain.

3. This is a _____ fit.

4. Tell me _____.

5. I _____ go to a movie.

6. The monster gave me a _____.

7. The plane had a good _____.

Not the Same!

Write the spelling word that means the opposite of each clue below.

8. day _____

9. give up _____

10. wrong _____

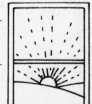

10

Level 6/Unit 1
Challenge Extension: Have children write pairs of questions
about any of the story characters, using *Who* and *Whose*.

3

Macmillan/McGraw-Hill

/ī/ -ight, -y

Proofreading Paragraph

Fix the mistakes in Anna's poem. Put in periods where they belong. Draw a circle around the words she spelled wrong. Spell them correctly on the lines.

Jinx, our cat, goes out each nite.   _____

He watches fireflies in their fliht   _____

He likes to try,   _____

I don't know wie,   _____

To give the little mice a frite   _____

Writing Activity

Add the correct spelling words to complete this ad for a magic wand.

Is your room a scary _____? Maybe your
parents cry, "Clean up that mess!" Our magic cleaning wand
_____ be what you need. Just give it a
_____. In no time at all, your room will be just _____.

Macmillan/McGraw-Hill

/ī/ -*ight*, -*y*

Test

One spelling word in each group is spelled correctly.
Draw a circle around the correct spelling.

1.	knite	nite	night
2.	tigt	tight	tiht
3.	suy	whi	why
4.	fright	freit	fryt
5.	wrighte	riet	right
6.	skie	sky	skigh
7.	fleyt	flight	flite
8.	slight	sliet	slieht
9.	tery	trigh	try
10.	might	myt	myte

Puzzle

Find five spelling words hidden in the fence around the house.
Draw a circle around each of them.

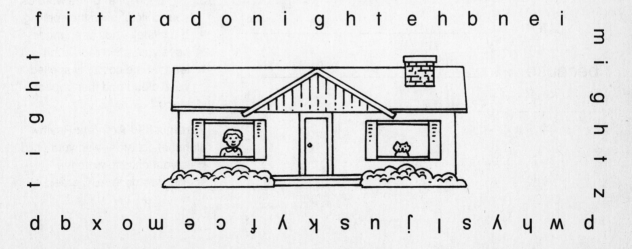

Macmillan/McGraw-Hill

/ē/-ee, -eam, -eet

1. street	1. _____
2. feet	2. _____
3. cream	3. _____
4. dream	4. _____
5. scream	5. _____
6. tree	6. _____
7. bee	7. _____
8. steam	8. _____
9. meet	9. _____
10. sweet	10. _____
Challenge Words	Challenge Words
after	_____
because	_____

Pretest Directions
Fold back your paper along the dotted line. Use the blanks to write each word as it is said to you. When you finish the test, unfold the paper and correct any spelling mistakes. Practice those words for the Final Test.

To Parents,
Here are the results of your child's weekly spelling Pretest. You can help your child study for the Final Test by following these simple steps for each word on the word list:
1. Read the word to your child.
2. Have your child write the word, saying each letter as it is written.
3. Say each letter of the word as your child checks the spelling.
4. If a mistake has been made, have your child read each letter of the correctly spelled word aloud and then repeat steps 1–3.

Parent/Child Activity: Review alphabetical order with your child. Help your child to write the spelling words in ABC order.

Macmillan/McGraw-Hill

/ē/-ee, -eam, -eet

Dog-ees

Look at the letter patterns on the collars of the dogs. Write the spelling words with those two patterns under the correct dog.

1. _____   2. _____

3. _____   4. _____

5. _____

6. _____

A Mix-Up

The letters in these spelling words are mixed up. Put the letters in order. Write the words on the lines. Then, draw a circle around the letters that are the same in all four words.

7. eamscr   _____   8. tseam   _____

9. craem   _____   10. dmear   _____

Macmillan/McGraw-Hill

/ē/-ee, -eet, -eam

Meaning Match
Read the words below.
Then, find the word in the box that means the same as those words.
Write the correct word on the line.

tree	scream	steam	bee	street

1. loud cry _____

2. insect that makes honey _____

3. tall plant _____

4. road _____

5. water coming from hot teapot _____

Quick Switch
One word in each sentence does not make
sense. Change one letter to make a
spelling word that makes sense.
Write the word on the line.

6. In my cream, my dog, Sassy, talked
   to me. _____

7. She told me to beet her at the
   pet store. _____

8. We sat on stools and ate ice dream. _____

9. Sassy said, "It tastes tweet." _____

10. I woke up and found her by my meet. _____

Challenge Extension: Have children write a set of directions explaining how to make
something or play a game, using the Challenge Words *after* and *because*.

Level 6/Unit 1

10

Macmillan/McGraw-Hill

/ē/-ee, -eam, -eet

Proofreading Paragraph

Some sentences ask something. They end with a question mark. Write a **?** at the end of each sentence that asks something. Write a **.** at the end of each sentence that tells something. Then, draw a circle around each word that is spelled wrong. Spell the word correctly on the line.

1. Why do you like honey _____

2. It is sweat and it tastes good _____ _____

3. Where do you find honey _____

4. First, I find a trea with a beehive in it ___Then I _____
   pull the honey out with my paw _____

5. Do the bese get mad _____ _____

6. Yes, but they do not hurt mee _____
   because my fur is thick ___

Writing Activity

Some of the words in the spelling list end with the same letters.
Write four sentences. Use two words that end with the same letters in each sentence. Use your best handwriting.

7. _____

8. _____

9. _____

10. _____

Macmillan/McGraw-Hill

/ē/-ee, -eam, -eet

Test

Draw a circle around each word that is spelled correctly.
Then, look at the words that are spelled wrong.
Write those words correctly on the lines.

1. steet _____
2. swete _____
3. meate _____
4. bee _____
5. creem _____
6. scream _____
7. feete _____
8. drem _____
9. tree _____
10. steam _____

Puzzle

Complete the crossword puzzle. Read each clue. Choose the answer
from the spelling words in the box. Write the answers in the puzzle.

| meet | street | bee | sweet | feet |

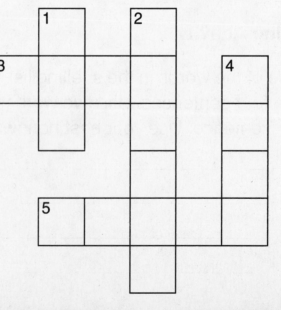

Across

3. Put shoes on these.

5. Sugar tastes ____.

Down

1. This flies and buzzes.

2. Ride on this.

4. See your friend.

Macmillan/McGraw-Hill

/ī/-*ike, -ime, -ite*

Pretest Directions
Fold back your paper along the dotted line. Use the blanks to write each word as it is said to you. When you finish the test, unfold the paper and correct any spelling mistakes. Practice those words for the Final Test.

To Parents,
Here are the results of your child's weekly spelling Pretest. You can help your child study for the Final Test by following these simple steps for each word on the word list:
1. Read the word to your child.
2. Have your child write the word, saying each letter as it is written.
3. Say each letter of the word as your child checks the spelling.
4. If a mistake has been made, have your child read each letter of the correctly spelled word aloud and then repeat steps 1–3.

Parent/Child Activity: Help your child discover the **i**-consonant-**e** pattern that repeats in all of the spelling words. Ask your child to name other words that make the same sound of **i** that you hear in **like** or **dime**.

1. _____	1. like
2. _____	2. time
3. _____	3. white
4. _____	4. bike
5. _____	5. hike
6. _____	6. strike
7. _____	7. dime
8. _____	8. lime
9. _____	9. kite
10. _____	10. write

Challenge Words

_____

_____

Challenge Words

know

no

Macmillan/McGraw-Hill

/ī/ -ike, -ime, -ite

Quilt Question

What is pictured on Jamal's quilt?
Color the quilt pieces with **ike** pattern words red.
Color pieces with **ime** words green.
Color those with **ite** words purple.

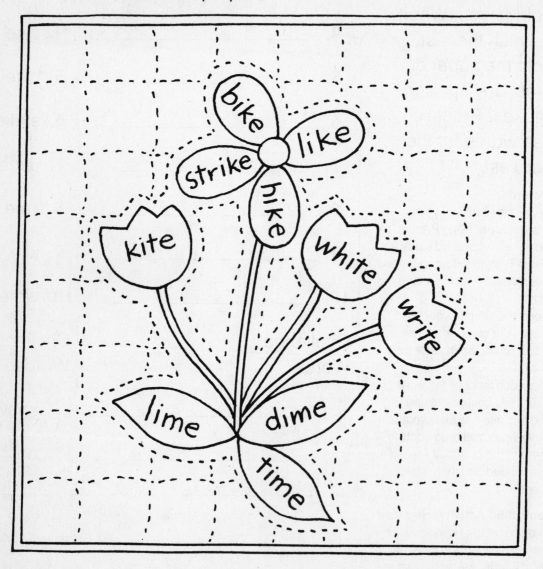

/ī/-ike, -ime, -ite

Time for Grandma

Which spelling words help to tell about something that's fun to do with Grandma?

Write the words on the lines.

1. We practice telling _____ on her old clock.

2. Sometimes we paint the _____ fence.

3. Grandma and I like to fly a _____ in March.

4. We _____ in the park.

5. We _____ each other letters.

Picture Perfect

What spelling word is the name of the picture?

Write it on the line below the picture.

6. _____   7. _____   8. _____

Macmillan/McGraw-Hill

8

Level 6/Unit 1
Challenge Extension: Have children take turns using *no* and *know*
in oral sentences. Have a volunteer spell the word each time.

13

/ī/-ike, -ime, -ite

Proofreading Paragraph

Draw a circle around the words that are spelled wrong. Write the words correctly on the lines. Then, put a period at the end of each whole thought.

> Dear Grandma,
>
> Dad is teaching me to play baseball I learned to striek the ball with the bat The ball hit a bush, and a wite rabbit ran out
>
> I lik the game very much and had a good tim
>
> Love,
>
> Ginny

_____ _____ _____

Writing Activity

Find the spelling word that answers each riddle. Write a sentence with that word in it below the riddle.

kite	dime	strike	lime

1. You can spend one or save one.

_____

2. I am a color, but also good to eat.

_____

3. I can fly if you help me.

_____

4. Make three of me and you are out.

_____

12

Macmillan/McGraw-Hill

/ī/ -ike, -ime, -ite

Test

Some extra letters have been added to the spelling words.
Draw a line through each extra letter.
Then, write the words correctly on the lines.

1. pdimex _____   2. whitke _____

3. hyike _____   4. wreite _____

5. allime _____   6. lieke _____

7. timee _____   8. kitte _____

9. stryike _____   10. bieke _____

Complete each rhyme by writing a spelling word on the line.

What I Like To Do

Ride my _____.

Take a _____.

Find a _____.

Eat a _____.

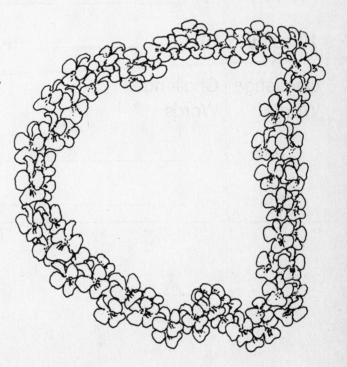

/ā/ -ait, -ay

1. wait	1. _____
2. day	2. _____
3. bait	3. _____
4. clay	4. _____
5. play	5. _____
6. sway	6. _____
7. gray	7. _____
8. pay	8. _____
9. way	9. _____
10. stay	10. _____
Challenge Words	Challenge Words
best	_____
most	_____

Pretest Directions

Fold back your paper along the dotted line. Use the blanks to write each word as it is said to you. When you finish the test, unfold the paper and correct any spelling mistakes. Practice those words for the Final Test.

To Parents,

Here are the results of your child's weekly spelling Pretest. You can help your child study for the Final Test by following these simple steps for each word on the word list:

1. Read the word to your child.
2. Have your child write the word, saying each letter as it is written.
3. Say each letter of the word as your child checks the spelling.
4. If a mistake has been made, have your child read each letter of the correctly spelled word aloud and then repeat steps 1–3.

Parent/Child Activity: Play a game with your child. See how many of the spelling words you use as you talk about your day. Put a star next to each word each time you use it. At bedtime, see which word was the "winner."

Macmillan/McGraw-Hill

/ā/-ait, -ay

Stair Steps

All the spelling words on this list have the vowel sound you hear in **may** and **wait.** Write the **ay** words that fit in the shapes. Circle the letters that are the same in each word. Then write the spelling words on the steps below.

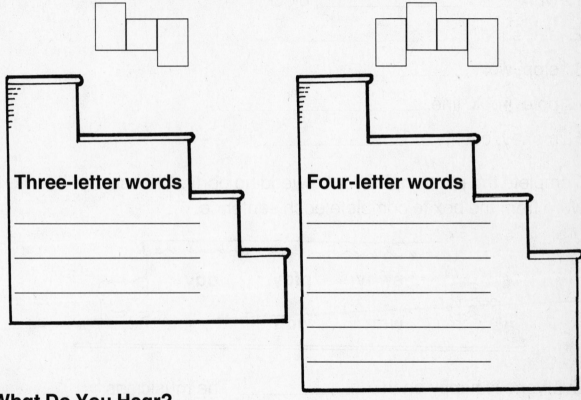

Three-letter words

_____

_____

Four-letter words

_____

_____

_____

_____

What Do You Hear?

Look at the words below. What letters make the vowel sound you hear in **straight?** Circle these letters in each word.

_____ wait _____   _____ bait _____

Macmillan/McGraw-Hill

/ā/-ait, -ay

Each group below is made up of words that go together, like a family. Add a word from the box to finish each word family.

gray	clay	stay	pay	bait

1. white, _____, black

2. dirt, sand, _____

3. stop, wait, _____

4. pole, hook, line, _____

5. money, cash, _____

Complete the paragraph about a wedding party. Choose a word from the box to complete each sentence.

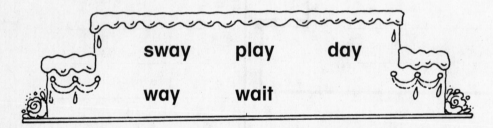

sway   play   day

way   wait

Everyone is happy on this _____. The musicians

_____ many dance tunes. The dancers step,

wiggle, and _____ to the music. We

_____ for the bride and groom to cut the cake.

 The bride throws her flowers all the

_____ across the room.

Challenge Extension: Ask children to complete these sentences: The best thing is _____ . I like _____ the most.

Level 6/Unit 1

10

Macmillan/McGraw-Hill

/āI/-*ait, -ay*

Proofreading Paragraph

Harry wrote a funny poem called a limerick. Help him fix his mistakes. Harry forgot to make some of the nouns plural. Add an **s** to make them plural. Then, circle the misspelled words. Write the words correctly on the lines.

A young fox went hunting one dey.   _____

He invited two duck ____ out to plai.   _____

Before he got thinner, he asked them to dinner.

Those duck____ ducked out, quacking
     "No wey!"   _____

Writing Activity

Find more **ay** and **ait** words on your spelling list. Write them on the blank lines. Then, write a paragraph about a make-believe wedding. Use at least four of the words you have written.

wait   stay   day   sway

_____   _____   _____

_____   _____   _____

_____

_____

_____

_____

Macmillan/McGraw-Hill

/ā/-ait, -ay

Test

Find the spelling word in each sentence. Circle it. Some of these words are spelled wrong. Write these words correctly on the lines.

1. I made a bowl out of cley. _____

2. Trudy has acted in a plai. _____

3. How late can you stay? _____

4. The graiy clouds soon blew away. _____

5. Wind made the branches sway. _____

6. Hansel and Gretel lost their weay. _____

7. It is hard to wayt for recess. _____

8. There are 24 hours in one deigh. _____

9. Dad will pay for our movie tickets. _____

10. Put some bate on your hook. _____

Puzzle

Find six spelling words with the vowel sound you hear in **day.** Circle them. Then write them on the lines.

```
w  o  h  g  r  a  y  e  l  s  m      _____
a  b  p  i  v  t  s  x  o  w  j      _____
y  z  i  w  r  y  k  c  l  a  y      _____
x  q  d  p  l  a  y  i  w  y  n      _____
s  t  a  y  e  o  f  l  w  e  t      _____
                                     _____
```

Macmillan/McGraw-Hill

CONTENT WORDS: SIMPLE IRREGULAR VERBS

Pretest

1. _____ 2. _____

3. _____ 4. _____

5. _____ 6. _____

7. _____ 8. _____

9. _____ 10. _____

Break the Code

Solve this message by writing these words in ABC order on the lines.

eat	come	should	can	hear	said

You _____ _____ to my house. We will

_____ peanut butter and jelly sandwiches. Did you

_____ my mother? She _____ that

you _____ be here tomorrow.

Macmillan/McGraw-Hill

CONTENT WORDS: SIMPLE IRREGULAR VERBS

Word List

1. said
2. went
3. are
4. can
5. shall
6. hear
7. should
8. fall
9. eat
10. come

Hunt n' Pick

Find list words in this puzzle. They may run across or down.
Circle them. Then write them on the lines.

```
w  e  k  s  j  s
e  a  n  h  f  a
n  h  e  a  r  i
t  m  u  l  z  d
x  f  a  l  l  o
```

_____   _____

_____   _____

_____

Proofer in Action

Proofread this report. Circle the words that are spelled incorrectly.
Then write them correctly on the lines.

Bugs Ar Your Friends

Bugs com with a bad name, but many of them cen help people.
Some eet bad bugs. We shuld be nicer to bugs.

_____   _____   _____

_____   _____

Macmillan/McGraw-Hill

REVIEW WORDS

Pretest

1. _____ 2. _____

3. _____ 4. _____

5. _____ 6. _____

7. _____ 8. _____

9. _____ 10. _____

Pattern Power!

Write the list words that have these spelling patterns.

ee	_____	_____
ight	_____	_____
ay	_____	

In the First Place

Which comes first in ABC order? Write the word in each pair that would come first in the dictionary.

like/kite _____
sweet/night _____
bee/hear _____
said/play _____

Macmillan/McGraw-Hill

REVIEW WORDS

Word List

1. bee	2. hear
3. way	4. flight
5. sweet	6. said
7. like	8. play
9. kite	10. night

What Does It Mean?

Write the list word that could match each dictionary definition. Check your answers in your dictionary.

After the sun sets _____

To listen _____

A sugary taste _____

Proofer in Action

Can you spot the spelling mistakes in these song titles and band names? Circle each word that is spelled incorrectly. Then write it correctly on the line.

Swete Liek Sally   by Flying Kyte

_____   _____

Dreams in the Nite   by Winona and the Waiy

_____   _____

When You Sed Good-bye   by Playe It Again, Sal

_____   _____

Macmillan/McGraw-Hill

/är/-ark, -ar

Pretest Directions

Fold back your paper along the dotted line. Use the blanks to write each word as it is read aloud. When you finish the test, unfold the paper and correct any spelling mistakes. Practice the words you missed for the Final Test.

To Parents,

Here are the results of your child's weekly spelling Pretest. You can help your child study for the Final Test by following these simple steps for each word on the list:

1. Read the word to your child.
2. Have your child write the word, saying each letter as it is written.
3. Say each letter of the word as your child checks the spelling.
4. If a mistake has been made, have your child read each letter of the correctly spelled word aloud and then repeat steps 1–3.

Parent/Child Activity: Have your child give you a spelling test, using words from a newspaper. Model the steps in learning to spell a word. Then, study the week's spelling words together.

1. _____	**1.** mark
2. _____	**2.** star
3. _____	**3.** park
4. _____	**4.** far
5. _____	**5.** bark
6. _____	**6.** dark
7. _____	**7.** car
8. _____	**8.** jar
9. _____	**9.** spark
10. _____	**10.** shark

Challenge Words

Challenge Words

_____ *can't*

_____ *isn't*

Macmillan/McGraw-Hill

10

Level 6/Unit 2

25

/är/ -ark, -ar

Solve Word Problems

All the spelling words this week have the vowel sound you hear in **bar** and **lark**. Add and subtract the letters you are given to make the spelling words with the **ar** and **ark** patterns.

1. farm - m = _____

2. part - t + k = _____

3. start - t = _____

4. park - p + sh = _____

Challenge:

5. sp + are - e + k = _____

Stars with Sparkle

Which stars have spelling words with the **ark** pattern? Circle each one.

bark   mark   fair   make   arm   stare   dark

Macmillan/McGraw-Hill

/är/-ark, -ar

Just for a Lark

The game directions need to be completed. Fill in each blank with a spelling word.

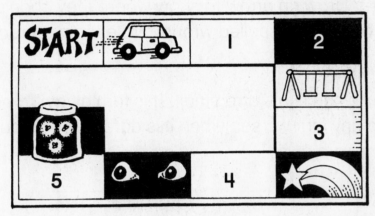

1. Take a _____ ride.

   Go ahead 3 spaces.

2. Play in the _____.

   Go back 2 spaces.

3. See a shooting _____.

   Go ahead 4 spaces.

4. Afraid of the _____.

   Go ahead 2 spaces.

5. Put fireflies in a _____.

   Go ahead 2 spaces.

Word Journal

Choose five words from this spelling list that you would like to use in a poem or story. Write them in your Word Journal. Add pictures you might use in your poem or story.

Macmillan/McGraw-Hill

5

Level 6/Unit 2

Challenge Extension: Ask children to complete the following sentences: I can _____, but I can't _____. He is _____, but he isn't_____.

27

/är/ -ark, -ar

Proofreading Paragraph

Help Josh with his science report. Some words are not in the right order. Draw an arrow to show where they should go. Then circle the words that are spelled wrong. Write them correctly on the lines.

    The sun is a starre small. It is farh away from earth. It looks bigger than any star we see when it is darck. That is because the other ones farther are away.

_____   _____   _____

Writing Activity

Finish Ali's story. Fill in the blanks with spelling words from the box. Then make up your own ending. Use words from the box.

mark	bark	park	dark	spark
car	jar	star	far	shark

I played with my dog, Lucky, in the evening. Soon it got

_____. Lucky chased after a _____. He did not

come back. Where could he be? Did he wander _____? We

looked and looked. No Lucky. We started home sadly. Then we heard

a _____ !

Macmillan/McGraw-Hill

/är/ -ark, -ar

Test

Circle the correctly spelled word to complete each statement.

1. A **sark/shark** lives in salt water.

2. Yellowstone is a national **park/pahrk.**

3. To start a fire, you need a **spark/spirk.**

4. Most people travel by plane and **kar/car.**

5. A real **star/stare** does not twinkle.

6. A felt-tip pen will leave a **mork/mark** on the table.

7. Two pints fit in a quart **jar/jeare.**

8. **Bark/barck** protects the tree trunk.

9. China is **fair/far** away.

10. The night is very **daurk/dark.**

Puzzle

Use the spelling words to complete the puzzle.

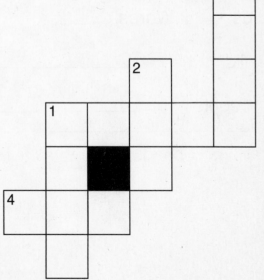

Across

1. A great swimmer

4. Drive a _____.

Down

1. Wish upon a _____.

2. Opposite of near

3. Dog talk

/ō/-ode, -ose, -ome

1. rode	1. _____
2. nose	2. _____
3. home	3. _____
4. dome	4. _____
5. chose	5. _____
6. hose	6. _____
7. close	7. _____
8. code	8. _____
9. rose	9. _____
10. those	10. _____
Challenge Words	Challenge Words
didn't	_____
people	_____

Pretest Directions
Fold back your paper along the dotted line. Use the blanks to write each word as it is read aloud. When you finish the test, unfold the paper and correct any spelling mistakes. Practice the words you missed for the Final Test.

To Parents,
Here are the results of your child's weekly Spelling Pretest. You can help your child study for the Final Test by following these simple steps for each word on the list:
1. Read the word to your child.
2. Have your child write the word, saying each letter as it is written.
3. Say each letter of the word as your child checks the spelling.
4. If a mistake has been made, have your child read each letter of the correctly spelled word aloud and then repeat steps 1–3.

Parent/Child Activity
Point out the vowel-consonant-vowel pattern for each spelling word. Say each word with your child. Ask your child to think of a rule for the **o** sound in these patterns. [The **o** sound is long when the pattern is **o**-consonant-**e**.] Ask your child what sound the **s** makes in **ose** words. [**z**]

Macmillan/McGraw-Hill

/ō/-*ode, -ose, -ome*

Every spelling word in your list this week has the vowel sound you hear in **close, home,** or **code.** Look at the words.

1. Which ending pattern is true for every word? Circle it.

vowel-consonant-vowel

vowel-vowel-consonant

consonant-vowel-consonant

Write the letters to show the three patterns of words in the list.

2. o _____ e   3. o _____ e   **4.** o _____ e

Look at each group of words below. Find the word that does not fit the pattern. Circle it.

5. code   chose   those   pose

6. rose   home   nose   hose

7. close   hose   rode   those

8. dome   those   home   Rome

Macmillan/McGraw-Hill

/ō/-ode, -ose, -ome

Make a poem! Fill in each blank with a spelling word.

1.  Each day my thirsty flower grows.
It's time to spray it with the _____.

2.  The butterfly stops beside the _____
to say hello and rest his toes.

3. **• • • ■ ■ ■ • • •** S O S Over the hills we quickly rode.
Could we find the secret _____?

Today, Yesterday
What spelling words show that the action happened in the past? Write the words on the lines.

Today I   **Yesterday I**

4. ride   _____

5. choose   _____

Picture This
What is a home? What is a dome? Use a dictionary to find out. Draw a picture of a home with a dome. Label the dome and the home.

"Home Sweet Dome"

Level 6/Unit 2
Challenge Extension: Have children write a
riddle using the words *didn't* and *people*.   6

Macmillan/McGraw-Hill

/ō/-ode, -ose, -ome

Puzzler

Choose the word from the box to complete the puzzle. Write the letters of each word in the squares, across or down.

rose	home	code	nose

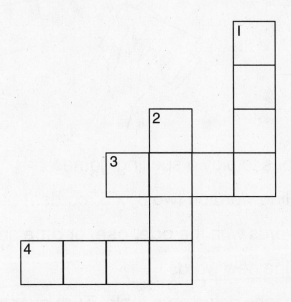

Across

3. To get to the bakery, just follow your _____.

4. I have to go _____ right after school.

Down

1. The sun _____, and the day began.

2. Secret messages are written in _____.

Macmillan/McGraw-Hill

/ō/ -ode, -ose, -ome

Unscramble the letters to make the spelling words that fit in each pattern.

Words with *ose*	**Words with *ode***	**Words with *ome***
sneo _____	dero _____	ehmo _____
sheoc _____	oecd _____	medo _____
theso _____		
heos _____		
cosle _____		
soer _____		

Follow these directions to play a spelling game.

1. Write each spelling word on two 3" x 5" cards.

2. Think of more words with the **ode, ose,** or **ome** pattern.

3. Make cards for the new words.

4. Put all the cards face down on a table. Turn over two cards.

5. If the words are the same, you take the cards.

6. If the words are not the same, turn the cards face down again. Your turn is over.

7. When all the cards are taken, the player who has the most cards wins.

Macmillan/McGraw-Hill

/îr/ -eer, -ear

Pretest Directions

Fold back your paper along the dotted line. Use the blanks to write each word as it is said to you. When you finish the test, unfold the paper and correct any spelling mistakes. Practice those words for the Final Test.

To Parents,

Here are the results of your child's weekly spelling Pretest. You can help your child study for the Final Test by following these simple steps for each word on the word list:

1. Read the word to your child.
2. Have your child write the word, saying each letter as it is written.
3. Say each letter of the word as your child checks the spelling.
4. If a mistake has been made, have your child read each letter of the correctly spelled word aloud and then repeat steps 1–3.

Parent/Child Activity: Point out that all of this week's spelling words rhyme. Encourage your child to make up a poem that uses all the words.

1. _____	1. year
2. _____	2. deer
3. _____	3. ear
4. _____	4. near
5. _____	5. cheer
6. _____	6. gear
7. _____	7. clear
8. _____	8. steer
9. _____	9. peer
10. _____	10. fear

Challenge Words

_____

_____

Challenge Words

things

think

Macmillan/McGraw-Hill

/îr/ -eer, -ear

All the spelling words in this list have the vowel sound you hear in **dear** John and **deer**, the animal.

Write the two patterns for spelling this sound.

1. _____   _____

Circle every spelling word with the **ear** pattern. Write those words in ABC order on the lines.

gear	steer	year	deer	ear
cheer	clear	fear	peer	near

2. _____

3. _____

4. _____

5. _____

6. _____

7. _____

Two of your spelling words name animals. What letters are the same in both of these words?

8. _____

Macmillan/McGraw-Hill

/îr/ -eer, -ear

What Is the Connection?

Write a word from the list to complete each pair of sentences.

1. A calf is a baby cow.

   A fawn is a baby _____.   year

2. Taste with your tongue.   deer

   Hear with your _____ _____.   near

3. Seven days are in a week.   ear

   Twelve months are in a _____.

4. **Big** is the opposite of **small**.

   Far is the opposite of _____.

Find the Missing Word

Use words from the box to finish each sentence.

fear	gear	cheer	steer

5. Stand up and _____ for our team!

6. The machine will not work without a _____.

7. I will push the wagon while you _____ it.

8. Some people have a _____ of high places.

Word Journal

Choose three words on your list to write in your Word Journal. Write the words in a sentence.

8

Level 6/Unit 2
Challenge Extension: Have children write and complete the following sentence: I like to think of _____ things, like _____ and _____.

37

Macmillan/McGraw-Hill

/îr/ -eer, -ear

Proofreading Paragraph

Can you find the misspelled words in Kate's story starter? Circle them. Then write them correctly on the lines. Kate also needs help putting in marks to show possession. Add the marks where they belong.

a deer**'s** eyes   (the eyes of the deer)

The first dir had no feer of Bear or Wolf. He also had sharp claws on his feet. He was very proud of his claws. The deers pride made the Great Spirit angry.

He said, "It is clere I must teach the deer a lesson. For one yier, I will give Bears speed to the deer and the deers claws to Bear."

Now the deer had to run from danger. He always had one eir turned to listen.

_____ _____ _____ _____ _____

Writing Activity

Write two sentences that describe the ending for Kate's story. See how many of the words in the box you can use.

fear	steer	ear
near	cheer	peer

_____
_____
_____

Macmillan/McGraw-Hill

/îr/ -eer, -ear

Test

Circle the correct spelling in each group.

1. year   yier   yaer
2. der   dir   deer
3. eer   ear   iar
4. knear   neer   near
5. cheer   chear   chire
6. girr   gear   geer
7. kleer   cleer   clear
8. steer   stiar   stear
9. pirre   peer   peare
10. fier   fear   feer

Puzzle

Find five spelling words that Tiger is thinking about. They may go across or down.

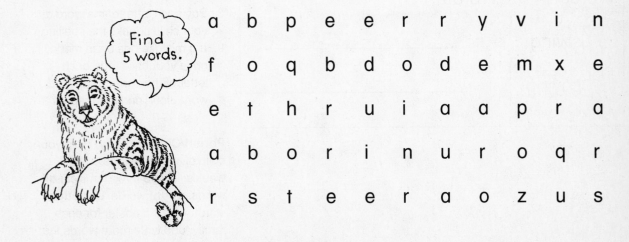

```
a  b  p  e  e  r  r  y  v  i  n
f  o  q  b  d  o  d  e  m  x  e
e  t  h  r  u  i  a  a  p  r  a
a  b  o  r  i  n  u  r  o  q  r
r  s  t  e  e  r  a  o  z  u  s
```

Find 5 words.

Macmillan/McGraw-Hill

/ô/ -all, -aught, -ought

1. all	1. _____
2. call	2. _____
3. taught	3. _____
4. brought	4. _____
5. caught	5. _____
6. ball	6. _____
7. tall	7. _____
8. small	8. _____
9. thought	9. _____
10. bought	10. _____
Challenge Words	Challenge Words
crying	_____
saying	_____

Pretest Directions
Fold back your paper along the dotted line. Use the blanks to write each word as it is said to you. When you finish the test, unfold the paper and correct any spelling mistakes. Practice those words for the Final Test.

To Parents,
Here are the results of your child's weekly spelling Pretest. You can help your child study for the Final Test by following these simple steps for each word on the word list:
1. Read the word to your child.
2. Have your child write the word, saying each letter as it is written.
3. Say each letter of the word as your child checks the spelling.
4. If a mistake has been made, have your child read each letter of the correctly spelled word aloud and then repeat steps 1–3.

Parent/Child Activity: Help your child divide the words on this week's list into three families: **all** words, **aught** words, and **ought** words. Make a poster for each family, and write more words that belong as you think of them.

/ô/ -all, -aught, -ought

Give It Your All

Four spelling words are made from the word **all.** Write them
on the lines below.

1. _____   2. _____

3. _____   4. _____

You OUGHT to Know

Make all the spelling words you can by matching the beginning sound
with the **ought** pattern. Write the words on the lines.

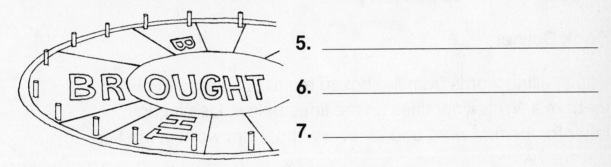

5. _____

6. _____

7. _____

Add letters to make spelling words that match the pictures.
Write the word beside the picture.

8. ? + aught   _____

9. ? + aught   _____

10. ? + all   _____

Macmillan/McGraw-Hill

/ô/ -all, -aught, -ought

Match-Ups

Draw lines from each spelling word to its meaning.

taught	round object
tall	paid for
bought	high
ball	explained, showed how
brought	carried to a place

Book Corner

Use spelling words from the box to make up interesting titles for books. Write your titles on the lines below. Use a capital letter for the first word and for every important word in the title.

all	call	caught	tall
ball	small	thought	brought

1. _____

2. _____

3. _____

4. _____

5. _____

Challenge Extension: Have children write a sentence for each Challenge Word, and then draw a picture to illustrate each sentence.

Level 6/Unit 2

10

Macmillan/McGraw-Hill

/ô/ -all, -aught, -ought

Proofreading Paragraph

Proofread Jack's letter to his brother. Names and the opening and closing words of a letter need capital letters. Add capital letters where they are needed. Then circle words that are spelled wrong. Write them correctly on the lines.

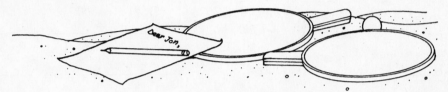

dear jon,

   When we went to the beach, uncle larry brot a game. He tought me to play. You use paddles to bat a smal, hard boll back and forth. The ball really flew, and so did I!

      The game is fun! I will teach it to you when I get home.

                                    love,
                                    jack

_____ _____ _____ _____

Writing Activity

Use the words below to add to Jack's letter. Tell what he thought about another game.

all	thought	bought	tall	caught	ball

_____

_____

_____

_____

Macmillan/McGraw-Hill

/ô/ -all, -aught, -ought

Test

Circle the letter or letters that are missing in the spelling word. Then write each word on the line.

1. ___ll   (a / o)   _____

2. ___all   (k / c)   _____

3. b___ll   (a / o)   _____

4. sma____   (le / ll)   _____

5. b____ght   (oo / ou)   _____

Write a spelling word to complete each sentence below.

6. The big man was
   very _____.

7. Mother Robin
   _____ her
   babies to fly.

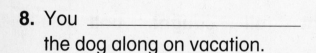

8. You _____
   the dog along on vacation.

9. She _____ of the right answer.

10. He threw the ball. I _____ it.

CONTENT WORDS: ADJECTIVES AND ADVERBS

Pretest

1. _____   2. _____

3. _____   4. _____

5. _____   6. _____

7. _____   8. _____

9. _____   10. _____

Sort It Out!

Unscramble each word and write it on the line.

tosm   _____

wysala   _____

htsi   _____

veenr   _____

selat   _____

Word Journal

The words on the list are useful for everyday writing. Copy those that are hard to spell in your Word Journal.

Macmillan/McGraw-Hill

CONTENT WORDS: ADJECTIVES AND ADVERBS

Word List

1. this
2. that
3. very
4. some
5. few
6. often
7. never
8. always
9. most
10. least

First Third

The first third of the dictionary covers the letters **A** to **F**. Write the list words that you would find in the first third of the dictionary.

_____   _____

Proofer in Action

Proofread each sentence. Circle the word that is spelled incorrectly. Then write it correctly on the line.

1. I know a fue people. _____

2. She is offen happy. _____

3. I allways like the snow. _____

4. Please pass me sum cheese. _____

5. I like thes party. _____

6. He seems vary nice. _____

Macmillan/McGraw-Hill

REVIEW WORDS

Pretest

1. _____   2. _____

3. _____   4. _____

5. _____   6. _____

7. _____   8. _____

9. _____   10. _____

Pattern Power!

Write each of the first eight list words on an index card. Then get ready to play a game of Memory Match! Mix the cards. Spread them out face down. Take turns with one partner turning up two cards. Do they have the same spelling pattern? If so, you keep the cards. If not, turn the cards face down, and your partner can try. Play until all the cards are matched. Whoever has the most cards WINS!

In the First Place

Which comes first in ABC order? Write the word in each pair that would come first in the dictionary.

tall/call   _____

dark/park   _____

year/near   _____

rose/nose   _____

Macmillan/McGraw-Hill

REVIEW WORDS

Word List

1. tall
2. call
3. park
4. dark
5. year
6. near
7. nose
8. rose
9. never
10. always

No Kidding!
Use list words to finish this silly rhyme.

This time last _____,

Spring was very _____.

I want to stay here in the _____,

And play with friends until it's _____.

I really wish that I were _____,

So I could reach the phone and _____.

Proofer in Action
Joshua's story has two spelling mistakes. Circle the words that are spelled incorrectly. Then write them correctly on the lines.

   The giant hit his noze because he was too tall for his doorway. This was the third new door he had made this yeer!

_____   _____

Macmillan/McGraw-Hill

/ü/-ool, -oon

Pretest Directions
Fold back your paper along the dotted line. Use the blanks to write each word as it is said to you. When you finish the test, unfold the paper and correct any spelling mistakes. Practice those words for the Final Test.

To Parents,
Here are the results of your child's weekly spelling Pretest. You can help your child study for the Final Test by following these simple steps for each word on the word list:

1. Read the word to your child.
2. Have your child write the word, saying each letter as it is written.
3. Say each letter of the word as your child checks the spelling.
4. If a mistake has been made, have your child read each letter of the correctly spelled word aloud and then repeat steps 1–3.

Parent/Child Activity: Use graph paper to make a simple word-find puzzle for your child. Encourage your child to create sentences for the words that are found.

1. _____	1. pool
2. _____	2. school
3. _____	3. soon
4. _____	4. spoon
5. _____	5. fool
6. _____	6. moon
7. _____	7. noon
8. _____	8. cool
9. _____	9. stool
10. _____	10. drool

Challenge Words

_____

_____

Challenge Words

there

they're

Macmillan/McGraw-Hill

/ü/-*ool*, -*oon*

Rhyming Time

Three of this week's spelling words have one letter before the letters **oon**. Write them on the lines below.

I. _____ 2. _____ 3. _____

What other spelling word rhymes with all three of these words? Write it on the line.

4. _____

A-MAZE-ing!

Help Tish, the Tadpole, swim through the maze pool. Use a crayon to color the path made by words that rhyme with **spool.**

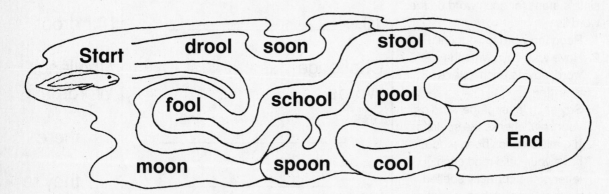

Macmillan/McGraw-Hill

/ü/-ool, -oon

Riddles to Solve

Use the spelling words in the box to answer these riddles.
Write the answers on the lines.

stool	moon	school	spoon

1. You need me to eat soup.   _____

2. You cannot fill me up, but once
a month I am full!   _____

3. I can stand on three legs or four.
I can hold you up for hours.   _____

4. When the bell rings, you walk
inside me.   _____

Rhyming Words

Use the picture clues to complete each sentence. Each part needs
two spelling words that rhyme. The words are found in the box. Write
the correct words on the lines.

noon	cool	soon	pool

5. Jump in the _____ and
splash. The water feels _____ .

6. Very _____ it will
be _____ .

Macmillan/McGraw-Hill

8

Level 6/Unit 3
Challenge Extension: Have children write a short fantasy story
about tadpoles, using the Challenge Words *there* and *they're*.

51

/ü/-*ool*, -*oon*

Proofreading Paragraph

Fix the mistakes below. Write a capital letter to begin the words for days of the week and months of the year. Then circle words that are spelled wrong. Spell them correctly on the lines.

   The park swimming puhl will open friday, may 20. Hours will be short until schole is out june 3. It will be open from 3:00 p.m. to 8:00 p.m. friday and from nun to 8:00 p.m. saturday and sunday. Park workers say the new water slide will sune be ready.

_____ _____ _____ _____

Writing Activity

Write a poem about a strange pet. Your pet can be a make-believe animal. Use rhyming words from the box to help you.

cool	drool	stool
fool	pool	

_____

_____

_____

_____

Macmillan/McGraw-Hill

/ü/-*ool*, -*oon*

Test

Circle the spelling word that is in each sentence. Some of the words are spelled wrong. Write these words correctly on the lines.

1. A dog may drul over a bone.   _____

2. You can sit on a stohl.   _____

3. The weather is cool.   _____

4. We serve lunch at nun.   _____

5. The moon is bright.   _____

6. A magician can fuhl you.   _____

7. Eat your pudding with a spun.   _____

8. New Year's Day is soon after Christmas.   _____

9. I go to skool all day.   _____

10. A pohl of water dripped on the floor.   _____

Many from One

Follow the directions to change the word **moo**. Watch the word become a different spelling word on each new line.

1. moo + n   ⟶ _____

2. moon - m + n   ⟶ _____

3. noon - n + sp   ⟶ _____

4. spoon - s - n + l ⟶ _____

5. pool - p + dr   ⟶ _____

Macmillan/McGraw-Hill

/âr/ -air, -are

1. square	1. _____
2. pair	2. _____
3. share	3. _____
4. scare	4. _____
5. dare	5. _____
6. chair	6. _____
7. stair	7. _____
8. repair	8. _____
9. flair	9. _____
10. fair	10. _____
Challenge Words	Challenge Words
each	_____
only	_____

Pretest Directions

Fold back your paper along the dotted line. Use the blanks to write each word as it is said to you. When you finish the test, unfold the paper and correct any spelling mistakes. Practice those words for the Final Test.

To Parents,

Here are the results of your child's weekly spelling Pretest. You can help your child study for the Final Test by following these simple steps for each word on the word list:

1. Read the word to your child.
2. Have your child write the word, saying each letter as it is written.
3. Say each letter of the word as your child checks the spelling.
4. If a mistake has been made, have your child read each letter of the correctly spelled word aloud and then repeat steps 1–3.

Parent/Child Activity

With your child, make up a rhyming poem about your day or about what you will do this evening. See how many spelling words you can use.

Macmillan/McGraw-Hill

/âr/ -air, -are

Walking on Air

All of the spelling words this week have the vowel sound you hear in **care** and **chair.** Follow the directions, and add letters to the word **air.** Write the six words on the lines.

1. p + air = _____

2. f + air = _____

3. ch + air = _____

4. st + air = _____

5. fl + air = _____

6. re + p + air = _____

I Dare You!

Find the three **are** pattern words that begin with an **s.** Write them in ABC order on the lines below.

7. _____   **8.** _____   **9.** _____

Write the **-are** spelling word that will fit in these letter boxes.

_____

Macmillan/McGraw-Hill

/âr/ -air, -are

Sound-Alikes

Write the spelling word that sounds the same as each word below.

1. pear _____   2. stare _____

3. flare _____   4. fare _____

Write a sentence using two words that sound alike.

_____

Word Journal

Pretend you own a fix-it shop. Pick four spelling words from your list. Write them in your Word Journal. Now use them in a paragraph telling about your shop.

_____

_____

_____

Wise Guys

Use spelling words from the box. Complete each piece of advice.

repair	fair	scare
share	chair	dare

5. We should _____. It is only _____.

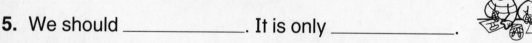

6. If you take a _____, you might get a _____.

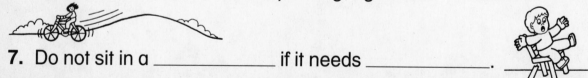

7. Do not sit in a _____ if it needs _____.

Macmillan/McGraw-Hill

/âr/ -air, -are

Proofreading Paragraph

Here is part of a play. Some nouns should be plural. They mean more than one. Add an **s** to fix these mistakes. Then, circle the words that are spelled wrong. Spell them correctly on the lines.

Lady: Eek! Who is there? Oh, Butler, you gave me such a skare.

Butler: Sorry, Madam. I came to tell you that another pare of silver candlestick_____ is missing.

Lady: What! Who would dair to steal from my castle?

Butler: Shh! Listen. Did you hear footstep_____ on the stairs?

_____ _____ _____

Writing Activity

Tell how to do one of these things:

Clean a spill off a chair.

Put on a pair of skates.

Repair a flat tire on a bike.

What do you do **first**? **second**? **third**?

Write the steps in 1-2-3 order on the lines below.

_____

_____

_____

_____

Macmillan/McGraw-Hill

/âr/ -air, -are

Test

Circle the correct spelling to complete each sentence.

1. A skware / square has four sides the same length.

2. It takes two to make a pair / parr.

3. Share / Shair the work to get it done fast.

4. Did the loud bang scare / scair you?

5. I dair / dare you to go to the haunted house.

6. Dad always sits in this chair / chehr.

7. The top stair / stahr creaks.

8. That car engine needs repare / repair.

9. They can dance with flair / flar.

10. When you play a game, play fair / fehr.

Game

Use the clues to fill in the blanks below.

1. sit on this   1. _____

2. to frighten   2. _____

3. to divide evenly   3. _____

4. a set of two   4. _____

5. to fix   5. _____

Macmillan/McGraw-Hill

/ā/ -ale, -ail

Pretest Directions

Fold back your paper along the dotted line. Use the blanks to write each word as it is said to you. When you finish the test, unfold the paper and correct any spelling mistakes. Practice those words for the Final Test.

To Parents,

Here are the results of your child's weekly spelling Pretest. You can help your child study for the Final Test by following these simple steps for each word on the word list:

1. Read the word to your child.
2. Have your child write the word, saying each letter as it is written.
3. Say each letter of the word as your child checks the spelling.
4. If a mistake has been made, have your child read each letter of the correctly spelled word aloud and then repeat steps 1–3.

Parent/Child Activity

Ask your child to sort the words on the spelling list into **ail** and **ale** columns. Have your child match the homophones (words that sound the same but are spelled differently) in the two columns.

1. _____	1. whale
2. _____	2. tail
3. _____	3. male
4. _____	4. rail
5. _____	5. pale
6. _____	6. fail
7. _____	7. sale
8. _____	8. snail
9. _____	9. tale
10. _____	10. jail

Challenge Words	Challenge Words
_____	their
_____	your

Macmillan/McGraw-Hill

/ā/ -ale, -ail

What Ails You?

All the spelling words this week have the vowel sound you hear in **nail** and **bale.** Write the word for each picture. Then circle each word that has the **ail** pattern.

1. _____

2. _____

3. _____

Silly Songs

The class made up titles for silly songs. Circle every word that uses the **ale** pattern.

4. One Pale Snail for Sale

5. The Sad Tale of the Lumpy Whale

Your One and Only

Only one spelling word will fit in this shape. Write the word.

6. _____

Macmillan/McGraw-Hill

/ā/ -ale, -ail

Use words in the box to complete each sentence.

male	tale	snail	whale	jail	pale

1. A _____ lives in the water.

2. A girl is a female, and a boy is a _____.

3. A tall _____ is a kind of story.

4. A _____ moves very slowly.

5. The game card said, "Go to _____."

6. The sick child looked _____.

Tricky Twins

Two of the words on this week's list sound just the same. They have different meanings and spellings. Write the tricky pair of words.

7. _____   _____

Now write the spelling word that sounds the same as this word:

8. sail _____

Word Journal

Write the tricky pairs of words in your Word Journal. Write the meaning beside each word. Think of more tricky twins to add to your list.

Level 6/Unit 3
Challenge Extension: Have children write sentences with each
of the Challenge Words, using the names of their friends.

8

61

Macmillan/McGraw-Hill

/ā/ -ale, -ail

Proofreading Paragraph

This ad for a nature video needs help. The writer forgot that the first word and all important words in titles need capitals, such as: "A Story of Two Friends." Write capitals where they are needed. Then, circle words that are spelled wrong and write them correctly on the lines.

"singing in the deep blue sea" is an amazing story. Watch divers as they follow the tal of a humpback wale. Marvel at the beautiful songs of a malle humpback named Humphrey. Will Humphrey's song help him find a mate? This taihl of love beneath the sea is now on sail at a store near you.

_____ _____ _____ _____ _____

Writing Activity

Write these titles correctly. Make sure the first word and every important word begin with a capital letter.

I. a tale of two cities

_____

2. hats for sale

_____

Macmillan/McGraw-Hill

/ā/-ale, -ail

Test

Unscramble each set of letters to make **ale** and **ail** spelling words.

ALE words		AIL words	
1. hawle _____		6. lita _____	
2. lame _____		7. ilar _____	
3. aelp _____		8. alfi _____	
4. alse _____		9. nilas _____	
5. tlea _____		10. alij _____	

Puzzle

Use the words in the box to complete the puzzle.

whale	sale	male
jail	snail	rail

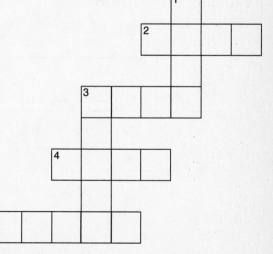

Across

2. A train's wheels run on a _____.

3. The price is less during a _____.

4. A law breaker may go to _____.

5. A _____ is a swimming animal

Down

1. A _____ redbird is more colorful than a female redbird.

3. You can find me creeping on a plant.

Macmillan/McGraw-Hill

/ē/-eel, -eed

1. eel	1. _____
2. weed	2. _____
3. feel	3. _____
4. need	4. _____
5. peel	5. _____
6. feed	6. _____
7. steel	7. _____
8. seed	8. _____
9. deed	9. _____
10. speed	10. _____
Challenge Words	Challenge Words
it's	_____
its	_____

Pretest Directions

Fold back your paper along the dotted line. Use the blanks to write each word as it is said to you. When you finish the test, unfold the paper and correct any spelling mistakes. Practice those words for the Final Test.

To Parents,

Here are the results of your child's weekly spelling Pretest. You can help your child study for the Final Test by following these simple steps for each word on the word list:

1. Read the word to your child.
2. Have your child write the word, saying each letter as it is written.
3. Say each letter of the word as your child checks the spelling.
4. If a mistake has been made, have your child read each letter of the correctly spelled word aloud and then repeat steps 1–3.

Parent/Child Activity

Ask your child to describe what is true about every spelling word in this list. [All have a double **e**. All have a long **e** sound.] Have your child make up rhymes, using the spelling words. Have your child correct the spelling of each word.

Macmillan/McGraw-Hill

/ē/-eel, -eed

What EEL Can Do

Three of your spelling words are made from the word **eel.** Write the words on the lines.

1. _____

2. _____

3. _____

What Is the Same?

What letters are the same in each of these words? Circle those letters. Now write the words in ABC order on the lines.

weed	feed	speed

4. _____

5. _____

6. _____

Pattern Perfect

Only one spelling word will fit in this pattern. Write the word in the letter shapes.

7.

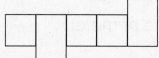

Macmillan/McGraw-Hill

/ē/-eel, -eed

Use the words in the box to fill in the missing words below.

1. Please do not _____

the _____.

peel
eel
feed
seed

2. A banana _____

An apple _____

What does each word mean? Draw a line to connect each word with its meaning.

3. need   something you do

4. speed   go fast

5. steel   a type of metal

6. deed   must have

Macmillan/McGraw-Hill

66

Level 6/Unit 3

8

Challenge Extension: Have children write sentences that include both Challenge Words.

/ē/-ee l, -eed

Proofreading Paragraph

Jeff watched minnows to see what they do. He made notes, like a good scientist. Now help him proofread. Every sentence should end with a period. It should begin with a capital letter. Circle words that are spelled wrong. Spell them correctly on the lines.

minnows fede on the plants in the pond Big fish try to eat them I saw one hide behind a water wead. The others all swam away with great speid.

_____ _____ _____

Writing Activity

Write a sentence for each group of words. Be sure to begin and end each sentence correctly.

 I. feel like dancing

_____

 2. a banana peel

_____

Macmillan/McGraw-Hill

/ē/-eel, -eed

Test

Circle the spelling word in each sentence. If it is spelled right, put a ✓ on the line. If it is spelled wrong, spell it correctly on the line.

1. Did you pick up the slippery eel? _____

2. Today we will weede the garden. _____

3. The kittens feal soft. _____

4. Babies need lots of love. _____

5. Please peale the apples for the pie. _____

6. Fish do not feed their babies. _____

7. That sword is made of stele. _____

8. A nut is really a seid with a shell. _____

9. A scout does a good deed each day. _____

10. The speide limit is 30 miles per hour. _____

Puzzle

Find five spelling words hidden in the fish pond. Circle them.

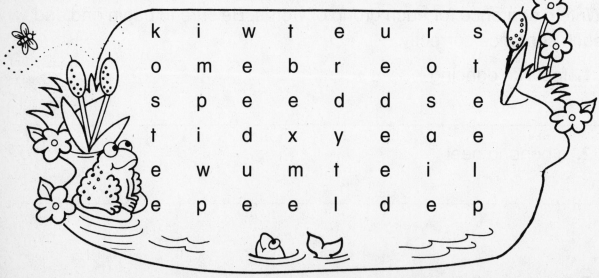

```
k  i  w  t  e  u  r  s
o  m  e  b  r  e  o  t
s  p  e  e  d  d  s  e
t  i  d  x  y  e  a  e
e  w  u  m  t  e  i  l
e  p  e  e  l  d  e  p
```

Macmillan/McGraw-Hill

Level 6/Unit 3

15

CONTENT WORDS: CONTRACTIONS

Pretest

1. _____   2. _____

3. _____   4. _____

5. _____   6. _____

7. _____   8. _____

9. _____   10. _____

Contraction Action

Don't is short for **do not** and **we've** is short for **we have**. An apostrophe (') stands for the missing **o** or **ha**. Put an apostrophe where it belongs in these words.

haven t	they ve	he s
aren t	I ve	it ll

Parting Words

The list words are contractions made up of words with **not**, **have**, **is**, or **will**. Write one of each type of contraction.

_____   _____

_____   _____

Word Journal

Choose five contractions from the list to add to your Word Journal. Write the two words that make up the contraction next to it.

Macmillan/McGraw-Hill

CONTENT WORDS: CONTRACTIONS

Word List

1. don't	**2.** won't
3. aren't	**4.** haven't
5. I've	**6.** he's
7. they've	**8.** we've
9. she'll	**10.** it'll

Negative Contractions

Some contractions are positive and some are negative. The positive words end with **'ll** or **'ve**. The negative words end with **n't**. Write all of the negative contractions from the list on the lines below.

_____   _____

_____   _____

Proofer in Action

Proofread this invitation. Circle the words that are spelled incorrectly. Then write them correctly on the lines below.

Iv'e been allowed to have a party on May 4 at 4 o'clock. Ask your mother if shell let you come. John said heis coming. Itw'l be lots of fun. Donet dress up! Weve planned a fun day.

_____ _____ _____

_____ _____ _____

Macmillan/McGraw-Hill

REVIEW WORDS

Pretest

1. _____ 2. _____

3. _____ 4. _____

5. _____ 6. _____

7. _____ 8. _____

9. _____ 10. _____

Pattern Power!
Write the list words that have each spelling pattern.

oo	_____	_____
are	_____	_____
ee	_____	_____

What's The Meaning of This?
Write the list word that matches each definition. Use the dictionary to check your work.

Skin of a fruit or vegetable _____

To frighten or become afraid _____

Part of an animal's body at the end _____

A story _____

Macmillan/McGraw-Hill

REVIEW WORDS

Word List

1. spoon
2. scare
3. don't
4. peel
5. tale
6. cool
7. he's
8. weed
9. tail
10. dare

Made in the Shade

Change the words below into list words by subtracting or adding the letters shown.

harpoon - har + s = _____

pail - p + t = _____

school - s - h = _____

wheel - w - h + p = _____

Proofer in Action

Proofread each sentence. Circle the word that is spelled incorrectly. Then write it correctly on the line below.

Do you know the tail about the king?   That movie will scair you.

_____   _____

I dropped the spoone on the floor.   I think hes really smart.

_____   _____

Macmillan/McGraw-Hill

/u̇/-ook, -ood

Pretest Directions

Fold back your paper along the dotted line. Use the blanks to write each word as it is said to you. When you finish the test, unfold the paper and correct any spelling mistakes. Practice those words for the Final Test.

To Parents,

Here are the results of your child's weekly spelling Pretest. You can help your child study for the Final Test by following these simple steps for each word on the word list:

1. Read the word to your child.
2. Have your child write the word, saying each letter as it is written.
3. Say each letter of the word as your child checks the spelling.
4. If a mistake has been made, have your child read each letter of the correctly spelled word aloud and then repeat steps 1–3.

Parent/Child Activity

Brainstorm words that have the vowel sound you hear in **book**. Encourage your child to label things at home whose names have this sound.

1. _____	1. look
2. _____	2. wood
3. _____	3. good
4. _____	4. hood
5. _____	5. took
6. _____	6. hook
7. _____	7. book
8. _____	8. cook
9. _____	9. stood
10. _____	10. shook

Challenge Words

Challenge Words

_____   ready

_____   daddy

Macmillan/McGraw-Hill

/u̇/-ook, -ood

All ShOOK Up

Find the words in the box that rhyme with **shook.** Write them on the lines.

book	cook	hook
good	hood	look

1. _____

2. _____

3. _____

4. _____

Riding on the -OOD Express

Send Caitlin's letter to her father on the path of **ood** words. Draw arrows to show your path.

took	hook	shook	
Start stood	book	look	End
good	wood	hood	

Macmillan/McGraw-Hill

/ủ/-ook, -ood

New from Two

Make new words by joining two words. Match each spelling word in Column 1 with a word in Column 2. Write the compound words you make on the lines below to go with the pictures.

Column 1	Column 2
1. cook	bye
2. good	land
3. wood	worm
4. book	out
5. look	book

1. _____

2. _____

3. _____

4. _____

5. _____

Macmillan/McGraw-Hill

10

Level 7/Unit 1
Challenge Extension: Have children write a sentence that uses both Challenge Words. Have volunteers read their sentences to the class.

75

/ù/-ook, -ood

Proofreading Paragraph

Jeri wrote a letter from camp to her parents. Circle words that are spelled wrong. Write them correctly on the lines.

June 17, 1997

Dear Mom and Dad,

    Scout camp is fun. Today we toake a hike. Then we cut woud to build bird feeders. We will canoe on the river tomorrow. I will kook a gud dinner over a fire.

                  Love,

                  Jeri

_____   _____

_____   _____

Writing Activity

Complete each sentence with words from the box.

cook	wood
hook	good

1. If you _____ a fish, I will _____ it for dinner.

2. The _____ smoke from the fire will make it taste

_____ .

Macmillan/McGraw-Hill

/u̇/-ook, -ood

Test

Circle the correctly spelled word to complete each statement.

I. How do these glasses luk / look on me?

2. Indians made spoons from wud / wood or bone.

3. This story was good / gould.

4. My coat has a hoode / hood.

5. I toock / took my bike on vacation.

6. Be careful of the sharp hook / hoack.

7. Our class made a bock / book about dinosaurs.

8. The meat should cook / koock for two hours.

9. I stood / stude in line to buy a ticket.

10. The dog shouck / shook water out of his fur.

Game

Write each spelling word on a separate 3 by 5-inch card. You can add review words, too. Put the deck face down. Draw a card. Ask the other player to spell this word. Take turns. Get a point for each word you spell correctly. The player with the most points wins.

Macmillan/McGraw-Hill

/ü/-ew, -ue

1. flew	1. _____
2. blue	2. _____
3. clue	3. _____
4. true	4. _____
5. blew	5. _____
6. knew	6. _____
7. dew	7. _____
8. stew	8. _____
9. crew	9. _____
10. glue	10. _____
Challenge Words	Challenge Words
alone	_____
along	_____

Pretest Directions

Fold back your paper along the dotted line. Use the blanks to write each word as it is said to you. When you finish the test, unfold the paper and correct any spelling mistakes. Practice those words for the Final Test.

To Parents,

Here are the results of your child's weekly spelling Pretest. You can help your child study for the Final Test by following these simple steps for each word on the word list:

1. Read the word to your child.
2. Have your child write the word, saying each letter as it is written.
3. Say each letter of the word as your child checks the spelling.
4. If a mistake has been made, have your child read each letter of the correctly spelled word aloud and then repeat steps 1–3.

Parent/Child Activity

Make up word cards for each of the spelling words. Place the cards, face down, on a table. Have your child match words in which the final sound is spelled in the same way.

Macmillan/McGraw-Hill

/ü/-ew, -ue

Birds of a Feather

All the spelling words this week have the vowel sound you hear in **new** and **blue**. Some words spell the sound with **ue**. Some spell the sound with **ew**. Write each word where it belongs. Then think of two more words for each group. Use a dictionary to check the spelling.

The UE Family

I. _____

2. _____

3. _____

4. _____

5. _____

6. _____

The EW Family

I. _____

2. _____

3. _____

4. _____

5. _____

6. _____

7. _____

8. _____

Macmillan/McGraw-Hill

/ü/-ew, -ue

Use words in the bowl to complete this paragraph.

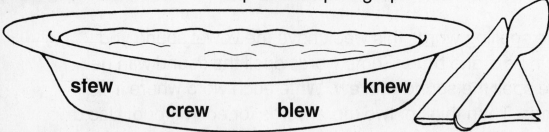

stew crew blew knew

My friends and I went to a football game. The cold wind

_____ in our faces. Everyone cheered. I just

_____ our team would win. At home Mom had

steamy, hot _____ and cider waiting. There

was plenty to warm the whole _____.

Opposites

Sometimes things are not the way they seem. Complete each
sentence with a spelling word to show opposites.

clue	true	knew	flew

1. I thought it was _____, but it was really false.

2. He said he _____ quickly home, but he really
   walked slowly.

3. She said she _____ my name, but she really
   forgot it.

4. The teacher said she would not give a hint, but she really gave us
   a _____.

Challenge Extension: Ask children to complete this sentence with the Challenge Words:
I asked my friend to come _____ with me, but I ended up going _____.

Macmillan/McGraw-Hill

/ü/-ew, -ue

Proofreading Paragraph

Adam's story is great, but it needs some corrections. When the action in a sentence happened in the past, use the **past tense.** Add **ed** to the verb. First, fix one of the verbs. Then, circle words that are spelled wrong. Spell them correctly on the lines. Last, add a period.

The queen's bluw diamond was missing! The police found no clew.

No one guess who the thief could be. But I—the queen's dog—I

new! Really it didn't matter. It was only made of glewe. How did I

know? I stepped on it and it stuck to me

_____ _____ _____ _____

Writing Activity

Pretend you are taking messages for a movie star. Write two messages you took for your boss. Use complete sentences, and include four spelling words from the box.

flew	blue	true	knew	crew

"While You Were Out"

3 P.M. From: _____

_____

3:30 P.M. From: _____

_____

Macmillan/McGraw-Hill

/ü/-ew, -ue

Test

Circle the spelling word that is spelled correctly.

1. flew / flue / flewe
2. clew / clu / clue
3. blewe / bleue / blew
4. doue / duew / dew
5. krew / crue / crew

6. blu / blue / blewe
7. true / tru / trew
8. nuw / knew / newe
9. stew / stue / sewe
10. glue / glew / gelw

Puzzle

Write the spelling word that goes with each clue. Then write the circled letters in the blank below to answer the riddle.

11. how a bird traveled ___ ___ ___ ⬭

12. a color ___ ___ ___ ⬭

13. a food ___ ___ ⬭ ___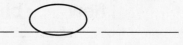

14. understood ⬭ ___ ___ ___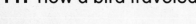

Why couldn't Sunday stop Monday from coming?

It was too _____!

Macmillan/McGraw-Hill

/är/ -art, -arm

Pretest Directions

Fold back your paper along the dotted line. Use the blanks to write each word as it is said to you. When you finish the test, unfold the paper and correct any spelling mistakes. Practice those words for the Final Test.

To Parents,

Here are the results of your child's weekly spelling Pretest. You can help your child study for the Final Test by following these simple steps for each word on the word list:

1. Read the word to your child.
2. Have your child write the word, saying each letter as it is written.
3. Say each letter of the word as your child checks the spelling.
4. If a mistake has been made, have your child read each letter of the correctly spelled word aloud and then repeat steps 1–3.

Parent/Child Activity

Ask your child to name words that rhyme with **arm** and **art**.

1. _____	1. arm
2. _____	2. part
3. _____	3. party
4. _____	4. alarm
5. _____	5. start
6. _____	6. cart
7. _____	7. dart
8. _____	8. farm
9. _____	9. charm
10. _____	10. harm

Challenge Words

_____

_____

Challenge Words

wishes

shoes

Macmillan/McGraw-Hill

/är/ -art, -arm

Every spelling word in this list has the vowel sound you hear
in **arm** and **art.**

1. What two letters are in every word?

   _____

2. All the words fit into one of two patterns. Fill in the missing
   letters to show the patterns.

ar_____   ar_____

ARTist

Color the shapes with **art** words to see the picture the artist made.

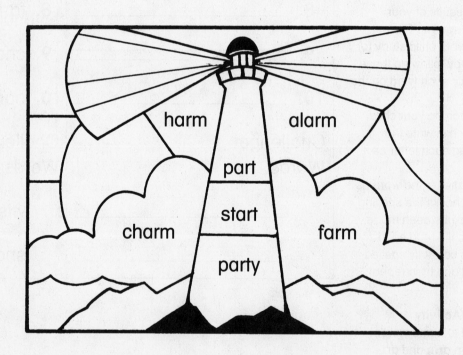

Macmillan/McGraw-Hill

/är/ -art, -arm

Puzzlers

Use spelling words in the box to answer each riddle.

start	alarm

1. When does an arm show a warning?

   When it is an _____.

2. What comes first and is made with **art**? _____

Word Journal

Pick four spelling words you want to know more about. Write them in your Word Journal in ABC order. Now look them up in a dictionary. For each word, write one or two meanings you did not know before. Try to use the words with their new meanings today.

Poet's Corner

Fill in each blank with a word from the box to complete the poem.

arm	part	charm	alarm

Some get their way with a strong _____.

Others, by using fright and _____.

I can't take their _____.

I believe from my heart

that it's better to win using _____.

6

Level 7/Unit 1
Challenge Extension: Have children use the Challenge Words to continue
the following story: Once upon a time, a shoemaker . . .

/är/ -art, -arm

Proofreading Paragraph

Kim wrote about bike safety. Proofread her paragraph and circle the words that are spelled wrong. Spell them correctly on the lines. Check the verbs to see if Kim added an **s** for singular verbs.

Right: Jimmy rides to school every day.

Wrong: Jimmy ride to school every day.

Jimmy ride his bike on the street. He wears his helmet. Jimmy

starts and stays on the right side. He uses his arhm to signal when he

turn. He does not dairt across the street in front of cars. He know how

to stay safe from herhm.

_____   _____   _____

Writing Activity

We pay attention to many signals every day. Write a paragraph about signals that help us stay safe. Use three spelling words from the list in your paragraph.

_____

_____

_____

_____

Macmillan/McGraw-Hill

/är/ -art, -arm

Test

Unscramble the words to show their correct spelling.

ART words		ARM words	
1. tarp	_____	6. ram	_____
2. typra	_____	7. raalm	_____
3. ratts	_____	8. marf	_____
4. crat	_____	9. mahcr	_____
5. tard	_____	10. hrma	_____

Puzzle

Use spelling words that fit
each definition to complete
the puzzle.

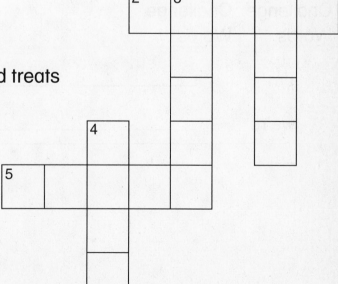

Across

2. a fun time with games and treats

5. something worn for luck

Down

1. begin

3. frighten

4. small wagon

Macmillan/McGraw-Hill

/oi/-oint, -oin, -oy, oil

1. boy	1. _____
2. point	2. _____
3. joy	3. _____
4. toy	4. _____
5. joint	5. _____
6. enjoy	6. _____
7. coin	7. _____
8. join	8. _____
9. boil	9. _____
10. soil	10. _____
Challenge Words	Challenge Words
I'm	_____
we're	_____

Pretest Directions

Fold back your paper along the dotted line. Use the blanks to write each word as it is said to you. When you finish the test, unfold the paper and correct any spelling mistakes. Practice those words for the Final Test.

To Parents,

Here are the results of your child's weekly spelling Pretest. You can help your child study for the Final Test by following these simple steps for each word on the word list:

1. Read the word to your child.
2. Have your child write the word, saying each letter as it is written.
3. Say each letter of the word as your child checks the spelling.
4. If a mistake has been made, have your child read each letter of the correctly spelled word aloud and then repeat steps 1–3.

Parent/Child Activity

Play "I'm Thinking Of" with spelling words. For example, you might say, "I'm thinking of something I might plant seeds in." (**soil**) Have your child say and spell the word with the /oi/ sound.

Macmillan/McGraw-Hill

/oi/-*oint*, -*oin*, -*oy*, -*oil*

Dragons of OI

Fill the dragons with spelling words that have each spelling pattern.

OINT

1. _____   2. _____

OIN

3. _____   4. _____

OIL

5. _____   6. _____

Pattern Smart

Write three more spelling words that have the same pattern
as **boy**.

7. _____   8. _____   9. _____

Circle the letters that spell the pattern.

10. Where do these letters appear? Underline the answer.

   at the beginning   in the middle   at the end

Macmillan/McGraw-Hill

/oi/-oint, -oin, -oy, -oil

All in a Set

Use a word from
the coin purse
to complete each set.

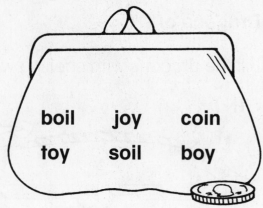

boil   joy   coin
toy   soil   boy

1. A male is a man or a _____.

2. A nickel or a dime is a _____.

3. In cooking you can bake, fry, or _____.

4. Earth is made of rocks, sand, and _____.

5. My favorite _____ is a doll or a ball.

6. Sadness and _____ are both feelings.

World Building

Be a word builder. Build two spelling words from the shorter
words by adding letters.

en + joy = _____   join + t = _____

Word Journal

Look up four of your spelling words in a dictionary. Write each
word in your Word Journal, along with its meaning.

Challenge Extension: Show how *I'm* and *we're* are formed. Then ask children
to suggest words to complete the sentence: I'm _____, but we're _____.

8

Macmillan/McGraw-Hill

/oi/ -oint, -oin, -oy, -oil

Proofreading Paragraph
Commas set off words in a list.

Example: We ate apples, grapes, and bananas.

Brianna interviewed her friend Julio. This is her article. Add any commas Brianna forgot. Circle any words that are spelled wrong. Write them correctly on the lines.

   Julio was born in Spain. He showed us a Spanish coyne called a centimo. In Spain they enjoi spicy food, bullfighting, and fiestas. A fiesta is a party with dancing food and games. Julio is a lucky boye to know about two countries.

_____   _____   _____

Writing Activity
Use a spelling word from the box to finish each sentence.

toy	point	join	soil	coin

Come _____ in the fun! Come to the Fun Fair!

Earn a _____ for every bag you throw in
Bozo's mouth.

Win a _____ every time at the fish pond.

Plant your own flower in a cup of _____. Only 25¢!

Guess how old the _____ is and win a prize!

/oi/-oint, -oin, -oy, -oil

Test

Circle the spelling word in each sentence. If it is misspelled, spell it correctly on the line. If it is correct, write a ✔ on the line.

1. A seven-year-old boey won the race.   _____

2. Point out your house to me.   _____

3. The choir sang "Joy to the World."   _____

4. Her favorite toie is a ragged jump rope.   _____

5. Your leg bends at the joynt.   _____

6. I injoy books about famous people.   _____

7. Have you ever seen a gold coyn?   _____

8. Please joune us for dinner Saturday.   _____

9. Does the water in a hot spring boil?   _____

10. Earthworms live in the soyl.   _____

Puzzle

Solve the puzzle. Circle five hidden spelling words.

```
b  c  a  x  e  n  j  o  y
o  t  o  y  s  t  u  p  m
i  g  e  j  o  i  n  t  u
l  f  r  a  i  o  i  d  k
v  u  w  o  l  n  s  a  f
```

Macmillan/McGraw-Hill

CONTENT WORDS: NUMBERS

Pretest

1. _____   2. _____

3. _____   4. _____

5. _____   6. _____

7. _____   8. _____

9. _____   10. _____

Dot-to-Dot

Write the number word next to each number. Then finish the dot-to-dot.

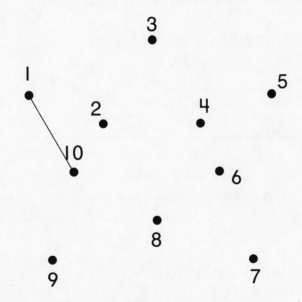

Word Journal

Copy the number words into your Word Journal and make a list of some times you might use them. Here are some ideas.

• to tell about your age

• to tell how many of something

• to tell about time

Macmillan/McGraw-Hill

CONTENT WORDS: NUMBERS

Word List

1. one
2. two
3. three
4. four
5. five
6. six
7. seven
8. eight
9. nine
10. ten

Different Order

Number order is different from ABC order. The words on the left are in ABC order. Rewrite them in number order.

ABC Order   Number Order

six   _____

ten   _____

two   _____

Plus Two

Solve the problems and write the answer words.

six + two =   _____

three + two =   _____

five + two =   _____

Macmillan/McGraw-Hill

REVIEW WORDS

Pretest

1. _____
2. _____
3. _____
4. _____
5. _____
6. _____
7. _____
8. _____
9. _____
10. _____
11. _____
12. _____
13. _____
14. _____
15. _____

Pattern Power!
Write the list words that have these spelling patterns.

| ew | _____ | _____ | _____ |

| art | _____ | _____ | _____ |

Homophone Hunt
Find a list word that sounds the same as each word below. Write the list words.

ate _____   flue _____

would _____   new _____

Macmillan/McGraw-Hill

REVIEW WORDS

Word List

I. flew	2. good	3. toy
4. crew	5. seven	6. wood
7. start	8. nine	9. boy
10. stood	11. dart	12. joy
13. knew	14. eight	15. cart

A Joyous Poem

Write these list words in ABC order to finish the poem.
toy   boy   joy

This is the _____ who got much _____

from his new _____ .

Proofer in Action

Proofread this science report. Circle the words that are spelled incorrectly. Write each word correctly above the circled word.

Today, we knu it was time to measure our plants in science

class. The teacher brought them out on a kart. We stoode a

ruler on end. One boiy had a plant that was sevin inches tall.

My plant was nien inches tall. I did a gude job with my plant!

Macmillan/McGraw-Hill

/ü/-oot, -oop

Pretest Directions
Fold back your paper along the dotted line. Use the blanks to write each word as it is said to you. When you finish the test, unfold the paper and correct any spelling mistakes. Practice those words for the Final Test.

To Parents,
Here are the results of your child's weekly spelling Pretest. You can help your child study for the Final Test by following these simple steps for each word on the word list:
1. Read the word to your child.
2. Have your child write the word, saying each letter as it is written.
3. Say each letter of the word as your child checks the spelling.
4. If a mistake has been made, have your child read each letter of the correctly spelled word aloud and then repeat steps 1–3.

Parent/Child Activity
Write the spelling words and other **oo** words on cards. Have your child say each word and sort the words into two stacks: those with the /u/ sound as in **scoot** and those with the /ù/ sound as in **look**.

1. _____	**1.** shoot
2. _____	**2.** scoop
3. _____	**3.** hoop
4. _____	**4.** loop
5. _____	**5.** snoop
6. _____	**6.** droop
7. _____	**7.** swoop
8. _____	**8.** boot
9. _____	**9.** root
10. _____	**10.** toot

Challenge Words

_____

_____

Challenge Words

while

which

Macmillan/McGraw-Hill

/ü/-oot, -oop

Can I Come, Too?

What answer does every younger brother or sister want to hear? Shade the parts of the puzzle that have **oop** words to find the answer.

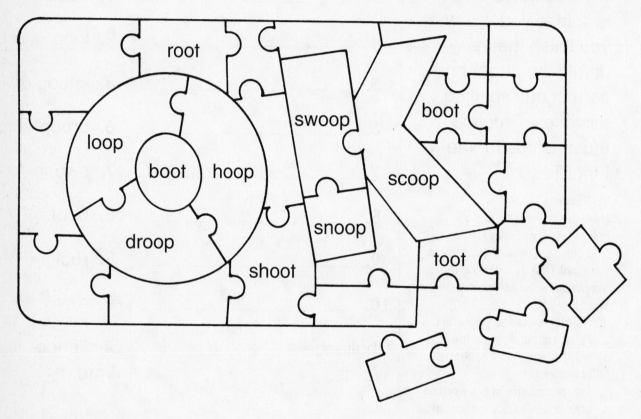

Find the Misfit!

Read each set of words. Circle the word that does not fit the pattern.

1. shoot, boot, book, root

2. swoop, scoop, snoop, stood

Macmillan/McGraw-Hill

/ü/-*oot*, -*oop*

Pair-Ups

These sentence pairs go together. Complete the second sentence in each pair. Use a word from the shoe that makes sense.

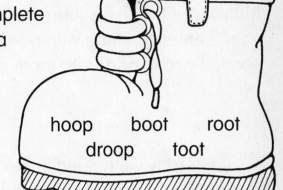

hoop   boot   root
droop   toot

1. Give a bell a jingle.

   Give a horn a _____.

2. Carry the football to the end zone.

   Throw the basketball through the _____.

3. Asparagus is a plant stem.

   A carrot is a plant _____.

4. With water, a plant stands up tall.

   Without water, it will soon _____.

5. A runner wears a tennis shoe.

   A cowboy wears a _____.

Word Journal

Pick four list words that you can use in a basketball poem. Write them in your Word Journal. Now write your poem in the Journal.

Macmillan/McGraw-Hill

6   Level 7/Unit 2
Challenge Extension: have children copy and complete the following sentence, using
the Challenge Words: _____ shoes should I wear _____ I clean the yard?

99

/ü/ -oot, -oop

Proofreading Paragraph

Matt wrote this in his journal. Check his writing for mistakes. Be sure each sentence starts with a capital letter. Circle any words that are spelled wrong and write them correctly on the lines.

yesterday we helped in the garden. We used a lupe of string to tie plants to stakes. then we watered plants that had begun to droup. We pulled weeds, too. One weed had a rute six inches long! When we finished, Mom gave us each a scoupe of ice cream.

_____   _____

_____   _____

Writing Activity

What is your favorite outdoor game? Write two sentences about it. Use two or more words from the word box.

shoot	scoop	hoop	loop	swoop	boot	toot

_____

_____

_____

_____

/ü/-oot, -oop

Test

One word in each pair is a spelling word that fits the pattern.
Circle the word that fits.

oot

shot / shoot

boot / boat

root / rote

toad / toot

oop

scope / scoop

hoop / hop

lope / loop

snoop / shop

sweep / swoop

drop / droop

Game

Make a card for each spelling word. Add more cards for other
words that fit the spelling patterns.

Pick a card. Think of a word that rhymes with your word.
Make a rhyme. If you can do this, you get to keep the card.
Take turns until all cards are drawn. Get a point for every card
in your stack. The player with the most points is the winner.

Macmillan/McGraw-Hill

/ô/ -alk, -aw

1. walk	1. _____
2. crawl	2. _____
3. saw	3. _____
4. chalk	4. _____
5. talk	5. _____
6. sidewalk	6. _____
7. beanstalk	7. _____
8. draw	8. _____
9. claw	9. _____
10. straw	10. _____

Challenge Words | Challenge Words

power _____

better _____

Pretest Directions

Fold back your paper along the dotted line. Use the blanks to write each word as it is said to you. When you finish the test, unfold the paper and correct any spelling mistakes. Practice those words for the Final Test.

To Parents,

Here are the results of your child's weekly spelling Pretest. You can help your child study for the Final Test by following these simple steps for each word on the word list:

1. Read the word to your child.
2. Have your child write the word, saying each letter as it is written.
3. Say each letter of the word as your child checks the spelling.
4. If a mistake has been made, have your child read each letter of the correctly spelled word aloud and then repeat steps 1–3.

Parent/Child Activity

Write each spelling word on a card. Think of other words you could add to them to make compound words. For example, **seesaw**. For words which are already compounds, think of new compound words that use the /ô/ portion of the word.

Macmillan/McGraw-Hill

/ô/-alk, -aw

Hopscotch Path
Which squares must you hop in to get to the end? Circle the squares with **alk** words to find out.

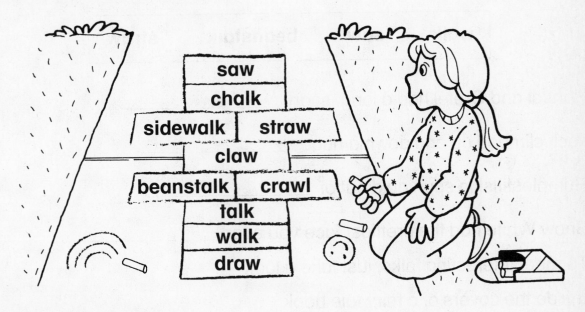

saw

chalk

sidewalk | straw

claw

beanstalk | crawl

talk

walk

draw

Scrambled Walk
Unscramble each set of letters to make a spelling word. Write the words in the bricks to complete the walkway.

1. was

2. wrad

3. lakt

4. wralc

5. slikdawe

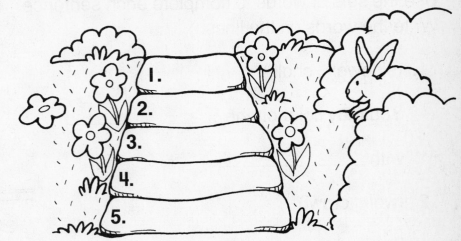

/ô/ -alk, -aw

Fairy Tale Folks

Use spelling words in the box to complete the poem.

walk	saw	beanstalk	straw

Hansel and Gretel had a long, scary _____.

Jack climbed up and down a huge _____.

Rumplestiltskin spun gold out of _____.

Snow White had the prettiest face you ever _____.

To meet interesting folks, just take a look

Inside the covers of a fairy tale book.

Use the sets of words to complete each sentence.
Write the words on the lines.

1. (sidewalk, chalk)

   You may color on the _____

   with _____.

2. (walk, crawl)

   Babies learn to _____ before they learn to

   _____.

Challenge Extension: To develop the meaning of the Challenge Words, ask children to name kinds of power (steam, wind) and tell what jobs they are good for.

Macmillan/McGraw-Hill

/ô/ -alk, -aw

Proofreading Paragraph

Neesha wrote a story. Check it for mistakes. Be sure **quotation marks** set off the speakers' words in conversation. Notice where commas, periods, and question marks go. Circle words that are spelled wrong. Write them correctly on the lines.

"Did you see what I just sauw?" asked Pat. _____

That man stole Mrs. Akia's purse! cried Matt.

The thin man dashed down the sidwak. _____

"Quick! You must cral under the fence!" _____
said Pat. "We can see if he runs up the alley."

Later the boys helped a police artist drae a _____
picture of the thief.

Writing Activity

The first word and all important words in titles need capital letters. Write the titles of these TV programs correctly on the lines.

1. A talk show for teachers: **chalk talk** _____

2. A class for sketch artists: **quick draw** _____

3. A show about going places:
   a walk across America _____

/ô/ -alk, -aw

Test

Circle the correctly spelled word in each group.

1. wolk / wauk / walk
2. crawel / crawl / craul
3. saw / sawe / sauw
4. chauk / chak / chalk
5. tok / talk / taulk
6. sidwalk / sidewak / sidewalk
7. benstalk / beanstok / beanstalk
8. drouw / draw / drawe
9. claw / clow / clau
10. staw / straw / strow

Puzzle

Write the spelling word in the space next to its meaning.

1. move on hands and knees   ○_ _ _ _
2. tool with sharp teeth   _○_
3. Jack climbed this.   _ _ _○_ _ _ _ _
4. make a picture   ○_ _ _
5. speak   _ _○_
6. walkway   _ _ _○_ _ _

Write the circled letters on the line below to answer this riddle.

The longer I live, the smaller I grow.

You can stop what I'm doing with just one blow.

What am I?   _____

Macmillan/McGraw-Hill

/ôr/ -or, -ore

Pretest Directions
Fold back your paper along the dotted line. Use the blanks to write each word as it is said to you. When you finish the test, unfold the paper and correct any spelling mistakes. Practice those words for the Final Test.

To Parents,
Here are the results of your child's weekly spelling Pretest. You can help your child study for the Final Test by following these simple steps for each word on the list:

1. Read the word to your child.
2. Have your child write the word, saying each letter as it is written.
3. Say each letter of the word as your child checks the spelling.
4. If a mistake has been made, have your child read each letter of the correctly spelled word aloud and then repeat steps 1–3.

Parent/Child Activity
Write the letters **ore** on a card so that they fill it. Write the consonant digraphs **sh, sn, st,** and **sc** on four other cards. As you say the spelling words made from these elements, have your child place the correct cards together and spell the word.

1. _____
2. _____
3. _____
4. _____
5. _____
6. _____
7. _____
8. _____
9. _____
10. _____

1. for
2. score
3. store
4. before
5. sore
6. more
7. tore
8. wore
9. shore
10. snore

Challenge Words

_____

_____

Challenge Words

born

torn

Macmillan/McGraw-Hill

10 Level 7/Unit 2

107

/ôr/-*or, -ore*

Sorting Words

Sort the **ore** words on the spelling list into these groups.

4-Letter Words	5-Letter Words
I. _____	5. _____
2. _____	6. _____
3. _____	7. _____
4. _____	8. _____

Word Builder

What spelling list word has only three letters?

9. _____

What six-letter spelling list word can you build using **for**?
Write the new word in the space provided.

10. be + for + e = _____

Macmillan/McGraw-Hill

/ôr/-*or*, -*ore*

It Happened When?

Use the words in the box to complete each sentence below.

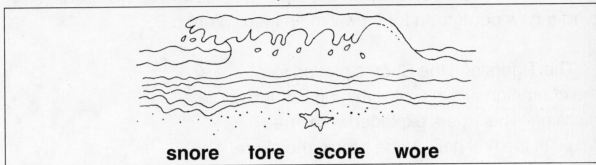

| snore | tore | score | wore |

1. My team cheers when I _____ a goal.

2. I _____ knee socks and shin guards to the game.

3. My mom says I _____ when I sleep.

4. I _____ the envelope open.

Who Am I?

One list word answers each riddle. Write the answers.

I meet the ocean.

I am the _____.

I am the number of points made by
each team in a game.

I am the _____.

Macmillan/McGraw-Hill

6   Level 7/Unit 2
Challenge Extension: For *torn*, compare the list word *tore*. For *born*, have
children complete this sentence: I was born in _____.

109

/ôr/ -or, -ore

Proofreading Paragraph

Read Peter's article about a soccer game. Circle the misspelled words. Write them correctly on the lines. Decide where he needs to start a new paragraph for a new main idea. Write a P.

   The Tigers and the Sharks played fore
the championship in a cold rain on Saturday
morning. The Tigers exploded with three
goals in the first half. At the break, the skore
was 3-0.   In the second half, the Sharks woke up. They tohr
into the Tigers' lead, scoring twice in two minutes. Just befor
the end, the Sharks made one last goal to tie the game.

_____ _____ _____ _____

Writing Activity

Write an ad for one of the products below. Use spelling words from the box to help you.

snore	sore	store	for	more	before	shore

Snore No More (a spray for the nose)
The Shore Express (A new bus that goes straight to the shore.)

_____

_____

_____

_____

Macmillan/McGraw-Hill

/ôr/ -or, -ore

Test

Add the missing letters to make spelling words that match the clues.

1. _____**or**_____ opposite of against

2. _____**ore**_____ make points

3. _____**ore**_____ a place to buy things

4. _____**fore**_____ opposite of after

5. _____**ore**_____ aching

6. _____**ore**_____ opposite of less

7. _____**ore**_____ ripped

8. _____**ore**_____ put on

9. _____**ore**_____ land by the water

10. _____**ore**_____ sound made when asleep

Puzzle

Complete the puzzle with spelling words.

Across

1. ahead of

3. put away for future needs

5. painful and tender to the touch

Down

2. Sing ___ your supper.

4. He ___ a hole in his shirt.

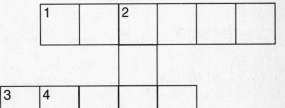

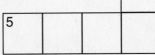

Macmillan/McGraw-Hill

/ō/-oast, -ow

1. show	1._____
2. yellow	2._____
3. window	3._____
4. rainbow	4._____
5. coaster	5._____
6. roast	6._____
7. toast	7._____
8. boast	8._____
9. grow	9._____
10. flow	10._____

Challenge Words

Challenge Words

beside _____

between _____

Pretest Directions

Fold your paper along the dotted line. Use the blanks to write each word as it is said to you. When you finish the test, unfold the paper and correct any spelling mistakes. Practice those words for the Final Test.

To Parents,
Here are the results of your child's weekly spelling Pretest. You can help your child study for the Final Test by following these simple steps for each word on the word list:
1. Read the word to your child.
2. Have your child write the word, saying each letter as it is written.
3. Say each letter of the word as your child checks the spelling.
4. If a mistake has been made, have your child read each letter of the correctly spelled word aloud and then repeat steps 1–3.

Parent/Child Activity
Have your child write a story using as many spelling words as possible. Give a star for every spelling word used and spelled correctly.

Macmillan/McGraw-Hill

/ō/-oast, -ow

Coast to Coast

What letters spell the vowel sound you hear in **coast**?

1. _____

What letters spell this same vowel sound in **glow**?

2. _____

The One-Syllable Club

Write the spelling words that have only **one** syllable. Group words with the same spelling pattern together.

ONE–SYLLABLE CLUB	
ow Words	**oast Words**
3. _____	6. _____
4. _____	7. _____
5. _____	8. _____

/ō/-oast, -ow

Draw a line from each spelling word to its picture. Then write
the words in ABC order on the lines below.

1. roast

2. window

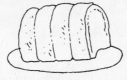

3. rainbow

4. toast

_____ _____ _____ _____

Not the Same

Write the spelling word that means its opposite in the blank
beside each item. Pick words from the box.

show   grow

5. shrink   _____

6. hide   _____

Macmillan/McGraw-Hill

Level 7/Unit 2
Challenge Extension: Have children draw pictures
and label them to illustrate the Challenge Words.

10

/ō/-oast, -ow

Proofreading Paragraph

Read Cory's rainy day poem. Circle any misspelled words.
Write them correctly on the lines.

I look out the windo while the rain comes down.

It's dreary and bleary and makes me frown.

Whatever happened to that warm, round fellow?

I want to tost in the sun's bright yelloaw.

Wait! There's a reinbow wiping up the gloom

And the sun sweeping raindrops like a giant broom.

_____ _____ _____

Writing Activity

Correct each sentence. Add capital letters and punctuation
marks. Add words if they are needed to make the sentence a
complete thought. Now write the sentences on the lines.

1. at the picnic, roast hot dogs and toast marshmallows.

_____

_____

2. is there yellow in a rainbow

_____

/ō/-oast, -ow

Test

Unscramble the letters and write each spelling word correctly.

ow Words

1. oflw _____
2. hows _____
3. wolyel _____
4. rogw _____
5. wwndio _____
6. wrinabo _____

oast Words

7. staro _____
8. boats _____
9. scoreat _____
10. tatos _____

Puzzle

Find your way out of the maze. Follow the path of the words that are spelled correctly.

1. show

2. window

3. toast

4. yellow

5. roast

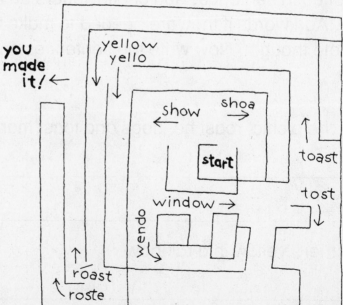

CONTENT WORDS: ADJECTIVES

Pretest

1. _____   2. _____

3. _____   4. _____

5. _____   6. _____

7. _____   8. _____

9. _____   10. _____

Antonyms and Synonyms

Antonyms are words that have opposite meanings, and synonyms are words that have the same meaning. Find two antonyms and two synonyms from the list.

Antonyms   _____   _____

Synonyms   _____   _____

Art Words

Artists know that mixing colors makes new colors. Use crayons or paints, and mix the colors below. Write the new color you make.

yellow + red = _____

red + blue = _____

Word Journal

Write the five color words from your list in ABC order in your Word Journal. Write the words again in order of your favorite color to your least favorite color.

Macmillan/McGraw-Hill

CONTENT WORDS: ADJECTIVES

Word List

1. orange   2. green

3. purple   4. pink

5. black   6. little

7. tiny   8. small

9. large   10. huge

Silly Poem

Use the list words to complete this poem. Try to make it as silly as you can.

Once there was a _____ tack.

His body was silver, his head was _____.

When he sat upon a big _____ ball,

The noise was big, the ball got _____!

Proofer in Action

Proofread these directions. Circle the words that are spelled incorrectly. Write each one correctly above the circled word.

Outline a larg drawing in blacke charcoal. Then paint the tini areas

with dark colors, such as browne. Light colors—blue and pinck—

should be next. Be sure to cover every litle space.

Macmillan/McGraw-Hill

REVIEW WORDS

Pretest

1. _____ 2. _____
3. _____ 4. _____
5. _____ 6. _____
7. _____ 8. _____
9. _____ 10. _____
11. _____ 12. _____
13. _____ 14. _____
15. _____

Pattern Power!

Write the list words that have these spelling patterns.

ore _____ _____ _____

aw _____ _____

Not the Same

Write the list word for each clue below.

not hide, but _____

not after, but _____

Today I see, but yesterday I _____.

REVIEW WORDS

Word List

1. shore	2. draw
3. window	4. green
5. scoop	6. before
7. saw	8. loop
9. orange	10. show
11. rainbow	12. straw
13. snore	14. droop
15. purple	

Fill in the Blanks

Write a list word on the line to finish each sentence.

We collect seashells by the _____.

I put a bright _____ sunflower on my window sill.

I _____ when I sleep.

On a beautiful summer day, the sun is shining and the grass is _____.

Easy as ABC

In each pair, circle the word that would come first in ABC order.

saw / draw   loop / scoop   window / rainbow

shore / orange   purple / snore   green / before

Macmillan/McGraw-Hill

/ou/-*out*, -*ouse*

Pretest Directions

Fold back your paper along the dotted line. Use the blanks to write each word as it is said to you. When you finish the test, unfold the paper and correct any spelling mistakes. Practice those words for the Final Test.

To Parents,

Here are the results of your child's weekly spelling Pretest. You can help your child study for the Final Test by following these simple steps for each word on the word list:

1. Read the word to your child.
2. Have your child write the word, saying each letter as it is written.
3. Say each letter of the word as your child checks the spelling.
4. If a mistake has been made, have your child read each letter of the correctly spelled word aloud and then repeat steps 1–3.

Parent/Child Activity

Create riddles with your child. Make sure that the answer to each riddle is one of the spelling words.

1. _____	**1.** out
2. _____	**2.** scout
3. _____	**3.** stout
4. _____	**4.** house
5. _____	**5.** shout
6. _____	**6.** sprout
7. _____	**7.** mouse
8. _____	**8.** blouse
9. _____	**9.** trout
10. _____	**10.** about

Challenge Words

Challenge Words

_____

mouth

_____

without

Macmillan/McGraw-Hill

/ou/-out, -ouse

Go All OUT!

Color in the shapes that have **out** words in them. You will see a picture.

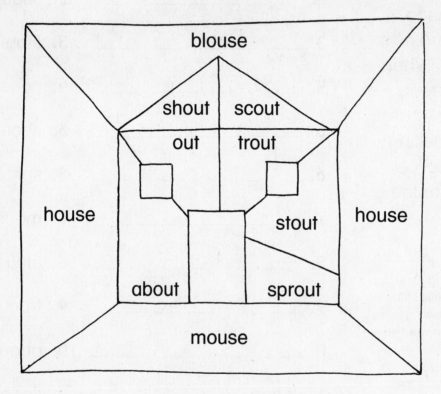

What picture did you color? _____

Write the other two **ouse** words on the lines.

I. _____

2. _____

Macmillan/McGraw-Hill

/ou/-out, -ouse

Complete each sentence using a word in the box.

trout	blouse	scout	sprout

1. Our guide will _____ for a good campsite.

2. The red _____ looks good with black pants.

3. Two weeks after planting, the seeds will _____.

4. A rainbow _____ is a pretty fish.

Colorful Words

People often use lively sayings that mean more than what each word alone means. They also like to compare things in fun, surprising ways. Write the spelling words to complete each saying.

house   mouse   shout

5. You are as quiet as a _____.

6. The theater had a full _____, so we couldn't get in.

7. Give me a _____ when you are ready.

Word Journal

Pick one of the sayings above. Write it in your Word Journal. Now write what you think it means. Give an example.

8 | Level 7/Unit 3
Challenge Extension: Have children write a silly rule or saying that uses both Challenge Words.

123

Macmillan/McGraw-Hill

/ou/-out, -ouse

Proofreading Paragraph

Jolynn wrote a paragraph about her favorite grown-ups. Did she use the verbs **is** and **are** the right way?

Rules: Use **is** with subjects that name one.
          Use **are** with subjects that name more than one.

Correct the verbs that are wrong. Then circle the misspelled words and write them correctly on the lines.

    My favorite grownups is my Grandpa Joe and my neighbors Mr. and Mrs. Chen. Grandpa Joe has a big laugh and are kind of stowt. He takes me oubt for ice cream and to the movies. I help the Chens weed their garden. The weeds sproat fast, so there are always more. The Chens are kind. They give me a present on my birthday.

_____   _____   _____

Writing Activity

Write a paragraph about a scout who tries to catch a trout. Use at least two spelling words to describe what happens.

_____

_____

_____

Macmillan/McGraw-Hill

/ou/-out, -ouse

Test

Complete each sentence. Circle the spelling word that is spelled correctly.

1. Can Lois come out / owte and play?

2. I would like to be a skout / scout someday.

3. The stout / stount clown played tricks and made us laugh.

4. Next summer we will paint the house / hoase.

5. A great shoute / shout went up from the crowd.

6. The corn has begun to sprout / spoute.

7. Where does a maus / mouse live?

8. Your blowse / blouse has five buttons.

9. Aunt Helen likes traut / trout fishing.

10. What is the story about / abawt?

Puzzle

Find five spelling words hidden in the house. Circle them.

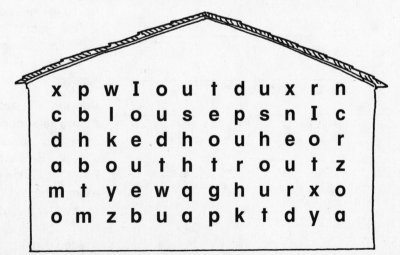

```
x p w I o u t d u x r n
c b l o u s e p s n I c
d h k e d h o u h e o r
a b o u t h t r o u t z
m t y e w q g h u r x o
o m z b u a p k t d y a
```

Macmillan/McGraw-Hill

/ē/ -eat, -eak

1. beat	1. _____
2. heat	2. _____
3. peak	3. _____
4. treat	4. _____
5. seat	5. _____
6. meat	6. _____
7. sneak	7. _____
8. speak	8. _____
9. beak	9. _____
10. creak	10. _____
Challenge Words	Challenge Words
tries	_____
flies	_____

Pretest Directions

Fold back your paper along the dotted line. Use the blanks to write each word as it is said to you. When you finish the test, unfold the paper and correct any spelling mistakes. Practice those words for the Final Test.

To Parents,

Here are the results of your child's weekly spelling Pretest. You can help your child study for the Final Test by following these simple steps for each word on the word list:

1. Read the word to your child.
2. Have your child write the word, saying each letter as it is written.
3. Say each letter of the word as your child checks the spelling.
4. If a mistake has been made, have your child read each letter of the correctly spelled word aloud and then repeat steps 1–3.

Parent/Child Activity

As you help your child study, make and use two sets of spelling word cards to play "Go Fish." Play in the usual way, except when a player asks another for a card. Each player must spell the word on the needed card.

Macmillan/McGraw-Hill

/ē/-eat, -eak

Up Pike's Peak

Climb the mountain by following the path of **eak** words. Draw a line from the bottom to the top.

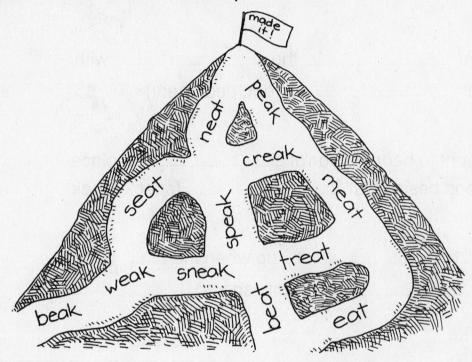

EAT 'Em Up

Two spelling words name things that are good to eat, and they contain the word **eat.** Write these two words on the lines.

1. _____

2. _____

Macmillan/McGraw-Hill

/ē/ -eat, -eak

Putting It Together

Use each set of words to complete the sentence. The pictures give you clues.

1. You can _____ the _____ with
this cool _____. (treat, beat, heat)

2. If you want to hear the parrot _____, place
some food beside his _____. (speak, beak)

3. It's hard to _____ up when the
stairs _____. (creak, sneak)

Sounds Alike

These pairs of words sound the same, but they have different spellings and meanings. Circle the spelling word in each pair. Then draw a line from the word to its definition. Use a dictionary if you need help.

peak/peek   to strike over and over

beet/beat   to make a squeaking sound

meat/meet   part of animal used as food

creek/creak   pointed top of a mountain

Level 7/Unit 3
Challenge Extension: Have children use the
Challenge Words to write a short rhyme.   15

Macmillan/McGraw-Hill

/ē/ -eat, -eak

Proofreading Paragraph

Janet wrote this paragraph about her great-grandmother for
Grandparents' Day. Did she use these contractions correctly?

can't = can + not   didn't = did + not

Fix any mistakes you find. Then circle the misspelled words.
Spell them correctly on the lines.

Great-Grandmother Hattie is ninety years old and a great lady. Mama
and I treet her with respect. Sometimes she cant hear very well.
That's why I try to spiek very clearly. I visit her at Palm Village. We
take a seate on a bench in the sun. She tells me stories about long
ago. I didn t know they traveled by wagon when she was little.

_____ _____ _____

Writing Activity

The words in this sentence are mixed up. Write the words in
the right order. Be sure the sentence begins with a capital
letter and ends with a period.

beat sun the mountain peak down on the

_____

_____

Macmillan/McGraw-Hill

/ē/-eat, -eak

Test

Circle the spelling word in each sentence. If it is spelled correctly, put a ✓ in the blank. If it is misspelled, spell it correctly on the line.

1. The drummer helps the band keep the beet.   1. _____

2. Will you please turn up the heat?   2. _____

3. There was a lot of snow on the mountain peeck.   3. _____

4. You should tret a cold with rest and soup.   4. _____

5. Please take a sete when the bell rings.   5. _____

6. Fish and meit are foods with lots of protein.   6. _____

7. I tried to sneak up on a bird and catch it.   7. _____

8. Try to spek clearly.   8. _____

9. Is a bird's beeke like a person's nose?   9. _____

10. Oil the hinges so the door won't creek.   10. _____

Macmillan/McGraw-Hill

/ā/-afe, -ave, -aze

Pretest Directions

Fold back your paper along the dotted line. Use the blanks to write each word as it is said to you. When you finish the test, unfold the paper and correct any spelling mistakes. Practice those words for the Final Test.

To Parents,

Here are the results of your child's weekly spelling Pretest. You can help your child study for the Final Test by following these simple steps for each word on the word list:

1. Read the word to your child.
2. Have your child write the word, saying each letter as it is written.
3. Say each letter of the word as your child checks the spelling.
4. If a mistake has been made, have your child read each letter of the correctly spelled word aloud and then repeat steps 1–3.

Parent/Child Activity: As you help your child study, you and your child can use the spelling words to make up silly sentences in which two words rhyme.

1. _____	1. graze
2. _____	2. save
3. _____	3. safe
4. _____	4. daze
5. _____	5. blaze
6. _____	6. shave
7. _____	7. gave
8. _____	8. wave
9. _____	9. brave
10. _____	10. maze

Challenge Words

Challenge Words

_____ riding

_____ getting

Macmillan/McGraw-Hill

/ā/-afe, -ave, -aze

Presto Chango

Change each word into two other spelling words. Add or replace letters as the clues suggest.

1. Change the first letter in **save** to make two other spelling words.

save _____ a v e _____ a v e

2. Change the first two letters and the fourth letter in **brave** to make another spelling word.

brave _____ a _____ e

Spin the wheel! Make five **ave** words. Add **br**, **g**, **w**, **s**, and **sh** to **ave**. Write the new words on the lines.

3. _____

4. _____

5. _____

6. _____

7. _____

Macmillan/McGraw-Hill

/ā/ -afe, -ave, -aze

Silly Sentences

Use a word below to complete each sentence.

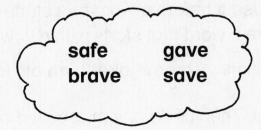

safe   gave
brave   save

1. If you want to _____ money, put it in the bank.

2. My parents _____ me a new bike for my birthday.

3. The police chief gave Tommy a medal for his _____ actions.

4. Wearing a helmet when riding a bike keeps you _____.

Lights, Camera, Action!

Words that show action in a sentence are verbs. Pick four verbs from the box. Write them in your Word Journal. Draw a picture illustrating each verb. Then write a sentence using the verb.

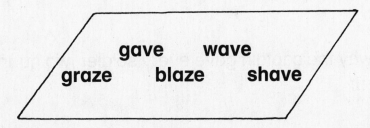

gave   wave
graze   blaze   shave

Macmillan/McGraw-Hill

8 Level 7/Unit 3
Challenge Extension: Have children identify the base word of each
Challenge Word, then write sentences using both forms of the word.

133

/ā/ -afe, -ave, -aze

Proofreading Paragraph

Fran wrote this letter to the editor of the newspaper. Did she know when to use **a** and **an**? Use **a** before a word that starts with a consonant. Use **an** before a word that starts with a vowel.

a good time   **an a**wful time   **a n**ew joke   **an o**ld joke

Fix any mistakes you find. Then circle any misspelled words. Write them correctly on the lines.

Dear Editor,

My family almost lost our home to a accidental fire. We forgot to turn off the lights one night. We woke up in a daz with smoke alarms going off and smoke pouring upstairs. A fire fighter said an old cord overheated and nearly set off a blaez. We sure were lucky.

Sincerely,
Fran

_____   _____

Writing Activity

Write each joke for a class book. Add capital letters, question marks, and periods where they are needed.

Molly: how do you know the ocean is friendly

Polly: It waves

Bo: Do you know why the captain gave every soldier two quarters before lights out

Joe: no.

Bo: they needed sleeping quarters

Macmillan/McGraw-Hill

/ā/ -afe, -ave, -aze

Test

Cross out extra letters to make spelling words that fit each pattern. Write each word correctly on the line.

ave

samve _____

shoave _____

gaive _____

wavoe _____

breave _____

aze

goraze _____

dazem _____

blaize _____

smaze _____

afe

stafe _____

Puzzle

Write spelling words that fit the definitions to complete the puzzle.

ACROSS

  2. to cut hair with a razor

  3. not afraid

  4. to move back and forth

DOWN

  1. to feed on grass

  3. to burn brightly

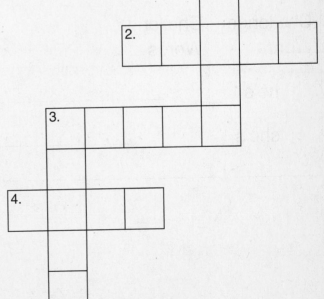

Macmillan/McGraw-Hill

/ou/-ound, -ow, -own

1. around	1. _____
2. found	2. _____
3. sound	3. _____
4. how	4. _____
5. down	5. _____
6. mound	6. _____
7. bound	7. _____
8. brow	8. _____
9. now	9. _____
10. brown	10. _____
Challenge Words	Challenge Words
he's	_____
she's	_____

Pretest Directions

Fold back your paper along the dotted line. Use the blanks to write each word as it is said to you. When you finish the test, unfold the paper and correct any spelling mistakes. Practice those words for the Final Test.

To Parents,

Here are the results of your child's weekly spelling Pretest. You can help your child study for the Final Test by following these simple steps for each word on the word list:

1. Read the word to your child.
2. Have your child write the word, saying each letter as it is written.
3. Say each letter of the word as your child checks the spelling.
4. If a mistake has been made, have your child read each letter of the correctly spelled word aloud and then repeat steps 1–3.

Parent/Child Activity

Have your child write each spelling word in a sentence. Then have your child find and circle the spelling word in each sentence.

Macmillan/McGraw-Hill

/ou/ -ound, -ow, -own

Throw One Out

Three words in each group have the same spelling pattern.
Circle the word in each group that does not fit the pattern.

1. sound, hound, brown, around

2. how, now, sew, cow

3. brown, brow, down, crown

4. ground, pound, bow, round

Write the words in the box in ABC order on the lines.

around   mound   found   sound   bound

5. _____

6. _____

7. _____

8. _____

9. _____

Write the pattern of letters that is the same in each word.

_____

Macmillan/McGraw-Hill

/ou/-*ound, -ow, -own*

Complete Leah's poem using the words below.

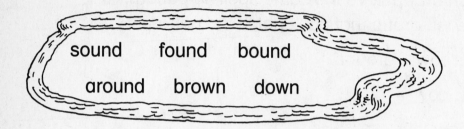

sound   found   bound

around   brown   down

Up on a mountain a stream can be _____.

It can't go up, so it travels _____.

It winds its way across and _____,

Through fields and forests green and _____.

It flows over cliffs with a thundering _____,

To reach the blue sea the stream is _____.

Word Journal

Pretend that you have found a dog. Find four list words that you
can use to tell what happened. Write the words in your Word
Journal. Now write sentences to describe what happened.

Challenge Extension: Have children write the two words that make up
each contraction, then write a sentence using each one.

6

Macmillan/McGraw-Hill

/ou/-*ound, -ow, -own*

Proofreading Paragraph

Alison wrote a note to send off in a bottle. She hopes she will make a new friend. Fix any mistakes in the note. First, see if she used **er** and **est** correctly. Add **er** to compare two things. Add **est** to compare three or more things.

My pencil is **big**, but yours is **bigger.**

His is the **biggest** in the classroom.

Also check for misspelled words. Circle them and write them correctly on the lines.

    Hello. My name is Alison. I am happy you have fownd my bottle. I wonder houw far it floated since I threw it into the Long Island Sond. Once I set off a balloon that went as far as Meriden. I hope this one will float farther than that.
    I am eight, and I live in New Haven, Connecticut, at I I I Lincoln Lane. I have broune hair, and I am the tallest one in my second grade class. Please write to me.

Love,
Alison

I. _____   2. _____

3. _____   4. _____

Macmillan/McGraw-Hill

/ou/-ound, -ow, -own

Test

Add the missing letters to make spelling words that match the clues.

1. ____ar____ on all sides
2. ____nd____ past tense of find
3. ____s____ something you can hear
4. ____h____ in what condition; to what degree
5. ____d n____ not up
6. ____m____ a pile or small hill
7. ____b nd____ certain; sure
8. ____br____ forehead
9. ____n____ at this time
10. ____br____ color made from red, yellow, and black

Puzzle

Find and circle five spelling words hidden in the bottle.

```
b g I s e b c a t s x
b r o w y r w p I o a
a e k a r o u n d u l
m z u d o w n f j n h
t y n v g n I m s d i
```

CONTENT WORDS: NUMBERS

Pretest

1. _____   2. _____

3. _____   4. _____

5. _____   6. _____

7. _____   8. _____

9. _____   10. _____

Pattern Power

Write five of the list words that end with the letters **ty**.

_____   _____

_____   _____

_____

Word Journal

Draw a number line in your Word Journal. Write five words from
the list in number order. Then write them in ABC order.

Macmillan/McGraw-Hill

CONTENT WORDS: NUMBERS

Word List

1. twenty	2. thirty
3. forty	4. fifty
5. sixty	6. seventy
7. eighty	8. ninety
9. hundred	10. thousand

Index Finger

Skim the index below. Write the number word that names the page on which each topic can be found.

eye, 24	finger _____
finger, 30	
foot, 50	foot _____
hand, 40	
head, 92	hand _____
knee, 53	
leg, 60	leg _____
mouth, 90	
	mouth _____

Proofer in Action

People won't come to the fair if they can't understand the sign! Circle and correct the words that are spelled wrong.

A hunderd things to do!   _____

A thowsand laughs!   _____

Adults over sicksty get in free!   _____

Macmillan/McGraw-Hill

REVIEW WORDS

Pretest

1. _____   2. _____
3. _____   4. _____
5. _____   6. _____
7. _____   8. _____
9. _____   10. _____
11. _____   12. _____
13. _____   14. _____
15. _____

Pattern Power!

Write the list words on the chart where they belong.

words with *eat*	words with *ound*	words with *ouse*

Word Journal

In your Word Journal, copy five list words that you have not yet written in the Journal. Write a sentence for each new word.

Macmillan/McGraw-Hill

REVIEW WORDS

Word List

1. mouse
2. house
3. blouse
4. meat
5. treat
6. seat
7. save
8. wave
9. gave
10. found
11. sound
12. around
13. sixty
14. seventy
15. eighty

Math Words

Write the list word that matches each definition.

Six tens _____

Seven tens _____

Eight tens _____

Puzzling Words

Eleven spelling words are hidden
in this grid. Circle the words
as you find them.

```
T  R  E  A  T  F  H  S  E
G  A  V  E  S  O  U  N  D
O  W  C  B  E  U  H  S  S
A  T  A  I  R  N  O  I  E
V  S  A  V  E  D  U  X  A
M  O  U  S  E  Z  S  T  T
X  B  L  O  U  S  E  Y  Y
```

Macmillan/McGraw-Hill